WOW GOD STORIES

38 AMAZING TRUE STORIES

DOUGLAS AND JANET HINCE

Self Published

All Scripture quotations are taken from the New King James Bible unless noted. Also note some Scriptures have been paraphrased.

Wow God Stories
38 Amazing True Stories

ISBN 979-8-218-10279-1
Copyright © 2022 by Douglas and Janet Hince
P.O. Box 23
Sartell, MN 56377
Phone 320-241-3892

PREFACE

I am a firm believer that this life is a journey and we do not travel alone. There is a mighty Father in heaven that walks with us in the hard times as well as the good. I have seen in Doug's life and mine how God has intertwined in our journey.

As we share some of the stories of God's blessings and protection in our life, our hope is that you would pause and look at the chapters of your life to see where He has intertwined in yours.

In some of the most difficult times, the times that may have rocked your world, if you look back, you will find that He was there the whole time. You may see how He helped you or blessed you even though at the time you could not see Him or experience Him. One thing that is true is He was there and continues to be there even now for you and for us.

Through our stories, we also hope you will be encouraged. We hope that you would find hope in knowing God is for us and with us always. He wants to be engaged and intertwined in our lives. He wants to walk the road of life here on this earth with us. He wants to bless us and help us, not only when we ask, but also when we don't think to ask.

Our walk with our Heavenly Father is one Doug

and I truly treasure. He is very close and dear to our hearts. We are forever grateful for all He has done for us. Be encouraged and enjoy a few of the stories from our life where God showed up in amazing ways.

LIST OF STORIES

DOUG'S TESTIMONY

I want to share my story of how I came to know God and how He has changed my life. I grew up in a normal family with a dad, a mom, a brother and two sisters.

We went to church as a family, but my heart wasn't in it. I went because my parents made us go. I never really knew if God was real or not. I knew other people believed He was real, but I didn't have a belief of my own.

When I was a teenager, I was hanging with the wrong people and started using alcohol and smoking pot, along with some other drugs. It took me down a wrong road, as that lifestyle usually will.

I got in trouble with the law, including a DWI and an open bottle, speeding tickets, and others. I was living my life for myself and didn't care much if it brought harm to others.

When I moved out of the house after high school, I was getting high, drinking daily and had a problem with substance abuse. I tried to quit several times but couldn't. I got married at 20 years old and had two kids by 23. I brought that lifestyle of using into my marriage and as you can imagine, it caused a lot of problems!

I was divorced at 27 and I was a mess. My life was out of control. I lost my wife, home and kids. I was broke and was an addict. I was able to visit my kids every other weekend, which isn't much, so it felt like I wasn't involved much in their life at all. The truth was, I wasn't, and I missed out on a lot of their life. I regret my selfish choices now. I really did want to spend time with my boys.

I knew I had a problem, so I checked myself into a hospital to go to drug and alcohol treatment. I didn't know a thing about getting sober, all I knew for the last 13 years my life revolved around getting drunk and stoned. I desperately needed help, or I was going to die an early death and I knew it. The treatment center told me I needed to have spiritual help and I thought, "don't bring religion into this mess I have enough on my plate."

I didn't know it's not about religion, it's about having a personal relationship with God. There is a big difference.

The treatment program lasted six weeks, and during the first week I had a small change of heart toward God. I thought to myself, "what I have been doing isn't working for me so maybe what the program is telling me to ask God for help is my answer to getting sober."

So, I opened my heart up a little and tried to embrace the thought that God was real, and He would help me. At the end of the six weeks as the program was ending, they told us some discouraging news. They said statistics show about one-third of us 28 people in the group will probably go back to using in the first month and about one-third will last a year and one-third might go on to live sober lives. It was devastating news to me, because I really wanted to learn to live sober. As I walked out to my car after the last day I thought, "now what?"

I didn't know it at the time, but God was working on my behalf. You see our lives are an open book to God. He knows everything about us and yet still loves us! He knew I would be in this mess at this time of my life and was waiting for me to surrender to ask for His help and repent of my selfish ways.

He spoke to my heart and told me to go see a pastor that had visited my home one year earlier. WOW. I didn't know it was a part of the plan but now a year later God would use that Pastor to speak into my life. He asked me if I ever prayed before? I said I really didn't know how or if I really believed it mattered? Our family didn't talk much at all about God or read the Bible or pray. We went to church and that was about all.

The Pastor encouraged me to give it a try, don't make it complicated, just talk to God and He will hear you. I thought I got nothing to lose I'm going to try it.

I was staying at my mom's house until I figured out my plan and one night I was praying the best I knew how, trying to talk to a God I couldn't see and didn't know if I even believed He was real. After I was finished praying I asked God are you even real? And can you help me? Please show me a sign that you are real. He touched me in my chest area and then I got body chills all over and I remember saying WOW God is real !!!!

I knew I had just experienced a touch from God. The next day I had a strong desire to read the Bible. Wow who would have ever thought that would happen to me.

I totally got delivered from alcohol and drugs , no longer was a battle for me!!!!! I started reading the Bible and learning about God and was getting answered prayers. That was 33 years ago and God has worked in my life so much and answered so many prayers. He told me to write this book to encourage people to pray and seek God and He will show up and work in your life too.

God is a Master at repairing, rebuilding broken lives. As a Christian you will still have challenges and trouble in your earthly journey but God will help you overcome. This life on earth is not the whole picture we have eternity to live, so really your 80-90 years here is only the beginning. God has completely changed the way I live, not that I never sin ever because truth is we all sin but I have a savior Jesus who I am accountable to and He is helping me to live a better life and to care about others and to help who I can.   God has allowed me to get married again and I have a daughter, step son, and 2 sons, I am sober, have a job, live in a nice home, vehicles, a boat, a motorcycle and some money in the bank.

God has completely restored my life!!!!!!   He will do the same for you if you let Him.

JANET'S TESTIMONY

I was raised in a home with a very ill mother and a father with a drinking problem. I was extremely close to my mother. I would say she was the one who taught me about Jesus. She used to read me stories about saints, as we were Catholic. One story was about a saint that was a child. She loved Jesus so much that she died young for him. I wanted to love Him that much, so I went to my room, knelt next to the bed and ask Him to come in to my heart. I really meant it. I was not just saying words. This began my relationship with Jesus.

Back to my family, between having babies and being ill, my mother was in and out of the hospital several times each year. The health concerns that caused the hospital visits were mostly due to blood clots and complications from Diabetes. I took care of my mother and helped her as she needed. My father seemed to be gone all the time back then, either working, going to the hospital or drinking. I was left to help my brother Joe watch over and raise our siblings. As a child, I was not close to my dad, and I blamed him for a lot of mom's problems, because my mother confided in me about things I probably should not have known as a child. My father was not very nice to me. I did not feel he loved or cared much for me. He treated me different than the others. The relationships between siblings were not healthy. There was physical fighting, yelling, and other unhealthy behaviors in our home. We did not have good boundaries.

As a child, I was very insecure, sad, confused, afraid and angry a lot of the time. I had a few friends. I liked music and our dog. My idea of play was when I did the housework, washed clothing with a wringer washer, hung them out on the clothesline, cooked and took care of my siblings. I pretended I was the owner of a large orphanage, and these were my children. I did not have much time to play. I remember one time when my mother was in the hospital and it was Christmas time. I was getting my siblings breakfast and making dad's lunch before the bus came. I was eight or nine years old. The coffee pot was too heavy, and I was trying to pour it into dad's thermos. I spilled it all over my arm and hand. Dad wrapped it and sent me to school. He told me to go to the nurse's office when I got there. I cried a good share of the day. I was not able to go to the Christmas party in my classroom because the burn was too bad and the pain was excruciating.

As a family, we made some good memories as well.

We had a yearly camping trip. My parents bought a ten-man tent and we would go to the lake for a week. Dad would go to work during the day and come spend the nights and weekends with us at the campground. We also went fishing a lot. It was fun and provided food for the family. Mom would take us swimming at a pool or lake when she felt good. There were always the trips to Como Park on Mother's Day each year. Mom loved going there for her special day. Christmas was a big to do at our house. Mom would make all kinds of Christmas cookies and treats with us kids. Dad would take all of us kids downstairs and we would take a bath or shower one at a time. We all got into clean pajamas and had to wait for everyone to finish their turn. Mom would be upstairs playing Santa. She would give dad some kind of a cue when she was done. We would all go upstairs to see if Santa had come. We would then sing Christmas Carols and open gifts. We always attended Christmas services. We spent Christmas at home with a full Christmas meal. Another fond memory was on Sunday's, dad would make fried chicken, put it in the oven, then we would go to church. He would finish preparing the meal after church and then we would eat. It was a meal we all looked forward to. Those are some of my fond memories.

In my life, I have experienced physical, emotional, and sexual abuse. This is hard for me to put in writing, but all of these things did lead me to Christ. I suffered from low self-esteem, deep hurts, a deep longing to belong and to be loved. I had hard lessons learned in relationships and experienced a number of broken hearts for men that I loved and trusted. After I left one such relationship with my son's father, I asked myself this question, "What is wrong with me that all these things happen to me in my life?"

Was I not good enough? Was I not worthy of love? No matter how good I treated people or helped people, I was always left behind. All I wanted was for someone to love me for who I am. I had a very unhealthy way of understanding love or receiving it. To me love never lasts and was full of disappointments.

I remember sitting on my bed talking to God. I said, "God, I do not know truly who you are. I have heard what people say about you, what movies and books say about you. If you get me out of the mess I have made in my life, I will learn about who you are and follow you the rest of my life." I moved out of my house in Hinkley and have not stopped following Jesus since. I have an amazing relationship with

Him now. He has brought healing to my heart, emotions, and physical being. I was able to forgive every person who had brought pain in to my life. I am free to love and be loved. He has taught me so many lessens in life and I am forever grateful. He put the right people in my path at the right time to show me the way. The LORD told me if I give him all my hurts and pain to Him, He will turn it and use it for good and He has.

God has restored my life and given me every desire I have. I now have a relationship with Him, a wonderful devoted Christian husband, a daughter that was promised to me, my three sons and their families. I have the ability to trust God and others. He healed my relationship with my father and gave me a deep understanding and respect for all he and my mother did for us. I have learned to see things through the eyes of my heavenly Father, the eyes of love! All it took was for me to surrender to Him and let Him lead the way.

GUN TO HEAD
DOUG

I am going to share a story of when God spared my life. It took place in my younger years of life as a teenager.

I wasn't a Christian at the time of these events in my life.

I knew about God, but didn't know God in a personal way. I went to church and heard about God, but really didn't understand anything about the Bible. Just going to church doesn't make you a Christian.

A Christian is someone who has received Jesus in their heart as their personal LORD and Savior, believing that He died for your sins, and that He rose again from the dead.

God wants everyone to be forgiven and saved, to spend eternity with Him in Heaven. However, we all have a free will and we choose whether we want God in our life or not. He will honor our choice!

The Bible says God knows who will receive Him and who will not receive Him as a personal Savior,

God knew that one day I would receive Jesus as my LORD and Savior and He kept me alive to be able to secure my eternal destiny.

I encourage you to read Psalm 139 it says *God knows everything about our life.*

As a teenager I got involved with alcohol and marijuana. I was living a life for myself; I didn't want God in my life. I only thought of Him as religious, and I didn't know Christianity was different then religion.

Christianity is *knowing God while religion is knowing about God.*

My friend and I were 15 years old at the time and we were hitch hiking to a beer party which was about 5 miles away. We put our thumbs out and got a ride by a person about 25 years old.

He seemed normal at first, and then things took a drastic turn for the worse within a couple of minutes.

We got out of town, and He was driving about 60 miles an hour and on purpose went off the road to scare us. We just about rolled the truck over at 60 mph. He did it a second time and we thought, "Wow, what is this guy's problem?"

He was high on something and told us he was dealing drugs and then thought we were going to turn him in to the police. We just wanted out and said, "Let us out and we will go our own way."

He pulled the truck over and it all happened so fast we didn't have time to think. Before we could get out of the truck, he reached in the glove box and pulled out a gun and put it to my head.

My first thought was I'm dead; he is going to kill me at age 15.

But God wasn't about to let that happen, I totally believe God wouldn't let him pull the trigger. Miraculously, he let us go after about 10 minutes. WOW, that was a close call to death. Praise God for his mercy!

I WILL FOLLOW YOU

JANET

I think most people who come to know the love of Christ come to Him through a difficult time in their life. This was true for me. Since I was a young child, I talked to Him. I had a relationship of some sorts with Him, but not a true understanding of who He was or is. I was 25 years old and came to a turning point in my life. I realized I made choices for myself that led me to a breaking point. I remember sitting on my bed crying, lost and alone. I reached out to God and told Him, but I did not know Him. I knew of Him: who people, church, movies and other sources said He was. I did not know Him personally. I told Him if he would get me out of the mess I, yes, I, created for myself that I would seek Him the rest of my life. I would find out who He was and follow Him the rest of my life. That was the beginning of a journey of love and trust in Jesus, my savior, guide and friend.

I moved to St. Cloud with my very young son. God put people in my path to help me, not only start over but discover a true walk with Christ. I repented for my lost lifestyle and gave my heart to Jesus. I started to go to church and started making better decisions.

I started by praying and asking for direction in everything. I did not trust I could make the right decisions. I saw a movie called "What about Bob" that helped so much. It was a movie about a man "Bob" who was fearful about everything. He had a counselor who told him to baby step it, to take life one step at a time. Bob did and was able to move beyond his fear. I baby stepped the next few years with God, my journey to a healthy relationship and lifestyle with Him. I met wonderful people going through similar issues.

I also discovered God. I spent time in the Bible looking for answers and encouragement. I went to counseling and dealt with childhood hurts and broken relationship issues. I started going to college, all part of the baby stepping it with God and life's decisions. It was not easy. There were ups and downs and more wrong choices as it is in life, but for the first time, I knew God and I knew He loved me then and loves me to this day. When I needed help or a clear direction for the next step, I asked Him first. He always showed me. Sometimes He showed me through another person, a song, His word or just His still small voice. My life is a life totally changed by the love of Christ and my seeking to know Him. I choose Jesus. He is very real to me, and He alone is my Savior.

Jeremiah 29:13 *And you shall seek Me and find Me, when you search for Me with all your heart.* (New King James) I sought Him with all my heart and He revealed Himself to me through His word, people, and His still small voice when I listen. I have and will continue to seek Him and follow Him the rest of my life.

BAR FIGHT

DOUG

This story is about a knife put to my chest from a bar fight in my younger days.

At this particular time, I was at the bar drinking as an 18-year-old. There were a lot of people there. This night club was known for not requiring ID for entry, so there were about a hundred people there, maybe more.

The bar had a dance floor, and they were playing music very loudly. The dance floor was crowded, with no extra room at all, so I was standing next to the edge of the dance floor talking to my friend. You had to be really close to each other to even hear each other talk.

There was a biker dressed in leather, dancing right next to me because of how packed the room was. He saw me standing next to my friend talking close to his ear so he could hear me, and the biker dude said, "Hey there faggot!"

I had been drinking for a while by this time, so my judgement was impaired. Without even thinking, I grabbed him by the coat and said, "What did you call me?" I was ready to fight right then and there.

Before I knew it within a couple of seconds, he pulled out a switch blade knife and put it to my chest, right by my heart and was pushing it firmly against me. He could have easily killed me stabbing me in the heart.

But by the grace of God, he didn't stab me, we shared some words of threats back and forth, but then it ended.

As you can see from these stories, God has protected me time and time again even in my stupidity. Even though I was out there making wrong choices, God is still merciful.

GOD'S FAVOR GROCERY SHOPPING

DOUG

Many years ago, when I first became a Christian, I was learning a lot about prayer. I never would have thought about praying about grocery shopping but now I know God wants to be involved in every area of our life.

I met a friend who had just become a Christian about the same time as me. We would have coffee together and talk about God and the Bible.

We would talk about the cool things God was teaching us, and it always seemed like Shirley was one step in front of me. By the way, Shirley was a friend I met after my divorce, and I hadn't met my wife Janet yet.

Shirley started telling me God was speaking to her and at first, I didn't understand it. I didn't think about the scripture that said Jesus is our shepherd and we are his sheep, and his sheep know and hear his voice.

It started to bother me. I guess I was jealous because

I wanted God to speak to me. He was, I just didn't recognize it yet. When I say God speaks to us, I don't mean an audible voice. He is Spirit, and He talks to our spirit. We must learn to listen to our heart, not our external ears.   I went to God in prayer and said, "why do you talk to Shirley and not me? I want to hear you talk to me too."

I waited with anticipation to have God speak to me, and nothing happened for a couple weeks. Then it happened! I will now tell you about how God spoke to me and told me to pray about my grocery shopping.

I was recently divorced at the time and had some financial challenges. I was paying child support and had to budget very carefully to pay my bills.

It was time for me to go grocery shopping. This was 30 years ago, and money went a lot farther when buying groceries. I had a $100.00 to go get some food and I couldn't go over, or it would mess up my budget.

I made a short list of a few items to get but didn't add it up and then was going out the door to go shopping. It was then that God spoke to my heart and said, "I want you to pray about your grocery shopping."

I stopped and was so surprised at first. I said, "God is that you?" I was so shocked that I was hearing from God but no one else was with me and I heard that voice loud and clear. I never thought about praying about grocery shopping ever before. I proceeded to go to the store and when I got to the parking lot, I prayed and asked God to bless my shopping that I would get what I needed and not go over my $100.00.

I started shopping and getting what I needed. I was about halfway done when I realized I bought some things I   didn't normally buy, like some spices. I didn't think much about it and kept shopping. I was finishing up and looked at my cart and I remembered I prayed, and I got upset at first because I thought I totally blew the budget. I thought this is way over $100.00.

The lady rang up the groceries and it cost me $100.00. It was actually a penny over but the lady threw in the penny so it was my $100.00 exactly!

I asked God why the penny over? He spoke to my heart and said, "You could believe that I just did a miracle, or do you believe it was just luck, chance, or coincidence?" I know He gave me answered prayer! He showed me I can hear from Him and He cares about every area of our lives.

FREE AIRLINE TICKET

DOUG

The favor of God is amazing. When God blesses a situation, it will turn out way better than you think. Ephesians 3:20 says: *God is able to do exceedingly, abundantly, above what we think or ask.* We have a part to play in the process of a prayer getting answered. We must ask and believe God hears us and will help us. Matthew 7:7 says: *ask, seek, knock.* Hebrews 11:6 says, *we must believe God is who he says he is and that he is a rewarder to those who diligently seek Him.*

In this story, I will tell you what happened when I prayed and asked for God's favor in getting an airline ticket to Texas. In 1993, I traveled to Israel for a 11-day trip. It was amazing and life-changing. It was my first time flying on a jet. I didn't know anything about airports or airlines, or how frequent flyer miles worked. When I flew on the Israel trip, I earned a lot of miles on my frequent flyer account. Like I said, I wasn't sure how that worked so I never even thought about using them.

My trip to Israel was in January of 1993. I went on

a trip there and came back home. I was so grateful for the opportunity to go. The last thing on my mind was thinking about another trip, especially the same year. It was July of the same year; I was talking to a friend about a large Christian convention put on by a ministry I was blessed by. I learned a lot about God from the ministry. I would go to the week-long meetings they have. I didn't even think it was an option to go. It was a large event that contained about 20,000 people. I knew it would be a fun time if I went.

My friend, said, "Doug, you should check into your frequent flyer points from your Israel trip."

At first, I thought, "I don't know how to check about it, do I just call the airport?" The week-long meetings were scheduled to happen in a couple of weeks from that point. I would have to get a hotel booked, get time off from work, and book a flight. I thought, wow, a lot of planning to do in a short period of time, but I was very excited at the thought of going. I prayed and asked God for help to make it happened. I said, "God, I don't know who I need to talk to or what to ask about the credit to get a free ticket. Please give me favor with the airline or the person I need to talk to."

I called and asked the airline representative about

getting a round trip ticket to Texas in a couple of weeks. First, he started to tell me all the reasons why that wasn't going to happen. He said I waited too long and that I don't qualify anymore. He said, even if I did qualify there is no way I would get the ticket in time to go in a couple of weeks. He was extremely stern about his decision on how it wasn't going to happen. When he was done telling me about it, I remembered I prayed for favor. I didn't say anything back to the gentlemen for a few moments. It was awkward on the phone, but I was giving God a chance to move in the guy's heart. I was shocked at what happened next. It was like a switch got flipped in the guy's reasoning. He said, I don't know why I am doing this. I have never done this before, but I am going to make it happen. I will get you the tickets in the mail and you will receive them in a few days.

I thought to myself, "Wow, God! You are so faithful!" God totally gave me favor and moved on that guy's heart to give me those tickets, just what I prayed for. I went to the convention and had a great time, thanks to God.

BIG BACK YARD

JANET

In my early 20's, I moved to St. Cloud for a life change. I had been living with a man, and we had an amazing son together, but the relationship was not working out, so I decided to leave. My son was 18 months at the time. I stayed with a friend for a few days and then went to a shelter for about a month. I really needed help and direction for my life.

I was very afraid of the unknown. I thought, "Where will my son and I live? How will I support him and myself? How will I live without his father? Who will help me?" I was all alone, or so I thought at the time.

I really sought God and asked Him for help. He placed many wonderful people in my path that gave me guidance and helped me to make healthier choices.

I was sitting in a chair wondering, "What is my next step? Do I go back to where I came from, or find a permanent place here to live?" I decided to stay in the area. I started to look for an apartment in the want ads. I remember praying and asking God for a place with a big back yard, so Jeremy would have a place to run and play. There it was; the heading that read **BIG BACK YARD**. I started to cry! God had heard my prayer! I called the number and got my first apartment. It was the lower level of a family's home. Ironically, it was a Christian family. That family became a large part of my support system to a whole new life.

Proverbs 3:6 says, *In all your ways acknowledge Him, And He shall direct your paths.* God directed my path all those years ago. One simple prayer for a big back yard led to many more steps forward with God!

BINGO

JANET

God will show up in unusual ways when you have a need. As a young single mom with winter fast approaching, I was in need of some things for the season. My son was three years old at the time. We both needed new coats, hats, and gloves for the upcoming winter season. I also need new tires on my car. I needed my car for my job that required me to make home visits to families. Sometimes I would travel up to 100 miles in a day, three or more times per week.

One evening, I was sitting at my kitchen table writing checks out for my bills and tithe to the LORD. I had just enough to pay them with nothing left over. I am a firm believer that God is faithful and will provide for all my needs, as I also pay tithes. I learned to trust in God for my every need. I sat back in the chair and told God, as He already knew, that I did not have enough for the tires or winter clothing. I told Him, "I figure it will be about $400." I was not sure how He'd provide it for me, but I am a thither and a good steward of my money. I was faithful to do my part, now He must do His. I reminded Him of two Bible verses; Philippians 4:19, which says, *And my God shall supply all your needs according to His riches in glory by Christ Jesus* and Philippians 4:6-7 which says, *Be anxious for nothing, but in everything by prayer and supplication, with thanksgiving, let your requests be made known to God; and the peace of God, which surpasses all understanding, will guard your hearts and minds through Christ Jesus.* This is the wording in the New King James Version. God has shown His faithfulness to me so many times that I knew He would show up, and He did.

I often went to visit and help my parents in Hastings, Minnesota. On one occasion, a good friend of mine talked me into going to play Bingo with her. I am not a big fan of Bingo, nor did I have the money to play. After much persuasion on her part, and her agreeing to pay for me to play, we went. We both agreed that if either of us won we would give the other person a 10-percent cut.

When we arrived, we found out there happened to be three larger pots that night, each being $400.00. I found that rather interesting, considering that is the exact amount I needed to provide winter clothing for me and my son. The first two came and went, both of which was split between three or four bingo players. I really did not give it much thought and kept playing. The last $400.00 game started. I called

Bingo on that game as the sole winner! I thanked the Lord for His provision and gave my friend the 10 percent that we agreed upon. After giving my friend $40, I had $360 left.

A few days later I went shopping. I bought the two winter coats, two hats, two pairs of boots and the mittens that we needed. I also bought the tires for my car and had them mounted and balanced. Guess what it cost? That is right, exactly $360! Coincidence? I think not. God is faithful to provide all my needs!

God will always provide in ways you do not even see coming. I am not suggesting that you go play Bingo or gambling to get your needs met. I am, however, saying to trust Him to get it to you in His way and timing. You will be amazed!

DEER HUNTING
DOUG

This story is about how God answered my prayer for venison meat.

I got divorced at age 27. I had two small children, both boys ages 3 and 5 at the time. I was given visitation rights every other weekend and vacation time to spend time with the boys.

I kept it a priority to not miss the visitation times with them, I didn't let anything take my time with my boys away.

I moved to St. Cloud after the divorce to take a job opportunity. I didn't want to move two and half hours away from them, but I was also overcoming alcohol and drug addiction at the time. I had to get away from that old lifestyle and start over new.

When I first moved to the St. Cloud area, I felt alone, as I did not know the area nor anyone nearby.

At the time, I enjoyed deer hunting. I would hunt with both a bow and a rifle, each in their own season.

Bow season started in September and rifle season was in November. This particular year, I wanted to go bow hunting. If a person doesn't get a deer with bow and arrow, there is another chance to hunt with a rifle in November, however you would have to buy your rifle license in September to apply for a doe permit. I bought both to be on the safe side.

The story gets interesting and complex. I was working a lot of overtime and couldn't get out bow hunting, so I asked my boss if he knew somebody who went bow hunting and could show me some places to hunt around the St. Cloud area. I figured I would eventually get out to hunt.

He said his friend Mike would probably take me out and show me where to hunt. I met him once before, and he said he would call me.

It was getting closer to the end of October, and I hadn't been out bow hunting yet, so I was looking at the November calendar to see which weekends were open for rifle hunting, but nothing seemed to work out.

I had two weeks to rifle hunt. The first weekend I had my boys so I couldn't go then. The second weekend I had to work. The last weekend I had my boys again. Although nothing seemed to be working, I prayed and said, "God you can figure this out. I pray that I get a deer and still see my boys and not to let my license go to waste."

One Sunday morning, I went to church. Mike had called me while I was at church. He left a message on my answering machine. (Yes, I still had a land line at the time 30 years ago!)

He said if I get this message in time before He left to go hunting that day, I could go with Him.

I got home, listened to the message and called Him right away but it was too late. He already left to go hunting.

At first, I was very upset that I missed the opportunity to go. I was saying out loud things like, "That figures I missed out! He probably won't get one anyways." I was expressing my anger and full of unbelief about what I prayed for earlier: That God would help me get a deer.

I was speaking contrary to what I had prayed earlier, and God was challenging me to get back in faith. I believed the Holy Spirit was helping me to change my confession back to faith-filled words.

I stopped complaining and instead turned back to my faith and said, "God I'm sorry for complaining and I ask for forgiveness. I pray Mike gets a deer today and not only gets one deer, but I pray he would get two deer and he would call me and ask me if I want to tag one."

After I prayed, I thought "WOW! That's a faith stretching prayer. You see, it isn't easy to bow hunt and get a deer and find it after you shoot it. Sometimes they run and you can't find them, so getting two in one day is abnormal, let alone Mike asking me if I wanted to tag one.

I went to bed that night and minutes later the phone rang, it was Mike. My heart was racing, I thought "WOW! Could my prayer be answered?"

He said, "Doug, this is Mike. I went hunting today and I got two deer, and I was wondering if you want to tag one?"

I thought, "God you are amazing!" Mike said that he had a close friend tell him that if he got an extra deer this year, he would like to have it and put his tag on it. However, Mike said, "I feel like I'm supposed to give it to you." He didn't have a clue that I had prayed for this all along.

Later, I shared with him that I am a Christian and I prayed that he would get two deer that day.

Mike said, "Well I'm glad somebody's praying for me!" He didn't realize God used him to answer my prayer.

In short, God gave me a deer, so I didn't waste my license. However, I still got to see my boys on the weekends. Praise God!

I was able to hunt more the following years. I encourage you to pray about every area of your life. God cares about you and loves you. He wants to be involved in everything you do. Don't miss out on this golden opportunity God freely gives you to know Him.

I encourage you to ask Jesus to make Himself known to you. I did and He has changed my life.

It is a great experience getting prayers answered. God wants you to know Him. He wants you to be a Christian, a child of God.

Read Romans 10:9-13 where it says *if you call on the LORD you will be saved, and Heaven will be your eternal home.*

PURPLE AND GREEN DOILY

JANET

Sometimes our Heavenly Father will ask us to do things we do not want to do to bless others. This story is one of my favorite stories about being obedient and blessing a stranger. Then I realized I was the one who would be blessed in return.

I worked one summer for a lady who was working for the Migrant Program in Bird Island, Minnesota. I was watching her daughter and my son while she was at the center. This particular day, I was watching them in the park. We were at a picnic table coloring in coloring books. There was a grandmother of some children from the Migrant Program sitting on a park bench watching them. There were about six children likely between 3 and 10 years old. This was in March and it was still cold out. She had a very thin summer-material type dress on. She had no sweater or jacket. She had a very bad cough, which sounded to me like she had pneumonia. I was worried about her, so I kept an eye on the children she was watching.

I am going to share something with you before I

continue the story. I attended SCSU University. I was very proud of this, as no one in my family at that point had attended a college. It was always my burning desire to have one of their sweatshirts of my own. I thought about it, dreamt about it, and was saving for it. One day, a friend of mine sent me a letter with $40.00 in it. She shared that she had been praying for me and God put it on her heart to send me this money. She shared that she believed there was something I want that God wanted to bless me with. I know without a doubt it was a SCSU sweat shirt. PRAISE GOD! Off to the book store I went. I got a SCSU sweatshirt for $40.00 even. It felt like Christmas and my birthday all in one day. I wore it with such pride!

Now back to Bird Island. On that day, I was wearing my SCSU sweatshirt. I had it for about 3 weeks. As I am working with the children, I hear that still small voice in my head say," Give her the sweatshirt". The battle in my mind was on. "No, it is mine you wanted me to have it."

Again, "Give her the sweatshirt."

"I will give her my jacket in the car, it will keep her warm."

I heard again, " Give her the sweatshirt."

I went to the trunk of the car and got my jacket out, with every intent to give the ill grandmother my jacket. I returned to the table and asked the oldest grandchild if his grandmother could speak English. He told me she could not. I ask him if he would interpret for me. His reply was "NO."

My response was, "No interpreting, no crayons and coloring books for you". He was not happy. He then agreed to interpret for me.

On our way to the bench, I asked him how long his grandmother had been sick. He said that she had been sick for a while and coughing up blood for a few days. I knew then that it was serious. When we got to the bench, I heard the LORD say, "Give her the sweatshirt." I asked the young boy to interpret word for word what I was about to say. I took off my sweatshirt and helped her put it on. I said," Jesus asked me to give you this sweatshirt to keep you warm." The boy looked at me like I lost my mind. I said, "Tell her word for word." He told her. I told him to tell her that Jesus is mindful of her and hears her prayers, that He loves her so very much and not to worry." The boy told her; she began to cry. Through the boy, she said she would give the sweatshirt back to me at the end of the day. I told her Jesus wanted her to have it, it was no longer mine, but hers. She said, "God bless you!"

I watched the children the rest of the day. She sat on the bench nice and warm. She continued to crochet. At the end of the day, the grandmother walked over to the table. She had something in her hand. She put a purple and green doily in my hands. She said, through her grandson, she prayed God would keep me there till she finished it. She told me when ever I look at it to remember her and pray for her.

I told the person I was working for the situation of the grandmother, when she returned. She set it up for her to see a doctor and receive medication.

That day I was so very blessed, I still after 30 years have the purple and green doily and the blessing that comes with listening to that still small voice. Years later, I was in a situation where I received 3 brand-new SCSU sweatshirts. I smile when I think about that. They no longer hold the meaning that it once did. I will forever remember and cherish the grandmother's doily of love and gratitude. I will remember when I bless others, I am the one who receives a better blessing. Paul said, in Acts 20:35 *"In everything I did I showed you that by this kind of hard work we must help the weak, remember the words the Lord Jesus himself said: 'It is more blessed to give than to receive."*

WALKING HER HOME

JANET

I had a lot of fears as a child. My greatest fear having an ill mother was that she would die. I use to have night terrors of this and daytime anxiety attacks. These started to occur about the age of 6 or 7 years old. They continued for years, I would scream and cry for long periods of time. The fear was so real, scary and terrifying.

When I was older, after giving my life to Jesus, I found reading the scriptures, praying and talking to God brought such peace. I was so close to her. I spent a lot of time with her. We shared so many personal things and one of the things we had in common was our faith. We spent a lot of time talking about God and Heaven. This brought both of us comfort and peace to press through her illness.

When I was in my mid 20's I would spend almost every weekend at mom and dad's apartment helping them. I mostly helped with house work, keeping mom company so dad could have a break. He would work all week and took care of her needs after work.

Mom and I would spend time sharing our faith

and doing what ever she wanted to do. She really enjoyed having Jeremy to tease and eat strawberries with.

Mom's health continued to decline. She struggled to walk any great distance, so we would push her in a wheelchair. She was getting weaker as time went on. I had the feeling she may leave us soon.

I remember praying and asking God if He would give her one good year, where she could do all the things she used to do. She loved to cook, bake, visit people, clean house and of course walk. If she could do all those things before her time here was done, that would be so awesome. Little did I know God would grant my request.

Mom got sick and went to the hospital, they sent her to rehab to gain strength before going home. She became very fearful and wanted out the facility. She became very mean to the nurses and staff. My dad called and asked me to call and talk to her because everyone was at wits end of what to do. Dad knew that if anyone could calm her down it was me. My dad told the nurse he would have me call.

When I called that evening the nurse told me she was waiting for my call and she informed me she would go bring my mom to the phone. While waiting for mom to come to the phone, I said a prayer asking God to talk to her through me. I was surprised by what I said when she got on the phone. I told her she had choices, she can fight the staff and be mean or she can be kind and grateful. Depending on her behavior, would be the deciding factor of how long she stays there. I told her, she needs to go to her therapy and do what was required for her strength building. She needs to be a light to others and go to the table for all meals and encourage those around her. I told her, she needs to say please and thank you to all the staff and encourage them too. I ended with do you understand me. She said, yes. I said, good I will call back tomorrow night to see if you're behaving. I told her I loved her and said goodnight.

The next evening, I called to check to see how things were going. The nurse said, "I do not know what you said to her last night. She is a different person. She put her call light the first thing in the morning to see if they would get her up. She had things to do". She told the staff she was sorry and said please and thank you to everyone all day. She went to therapy and asked if she could go twice. The nurse was so amazed by the change in her.

When I talked to her on the phone she said, "You are not going to believe this, Jesus appeared to me at the foot of my bed last night. He said, "It is not your time yet. I have things for you to do."

She continued to do all the things they required her to do. She was released form the rehab in about 3 weeks. The doctor was amazed he told my dad he thought she would be there for 3 to 6 months.

When she returned home, she rode her little scooter to the nursing home down the street. She would visit people there to encourage them. She cooked meals for dad, did dishes and light housekeeping. She was so excited and enjoyed sharing with others about her experience with Jesus. She was so proud. I was so proud of her. She was back to the person she was years ago. Not totally healed but alive, living and excited about the things she was doing.

About a year later I was driving to another town when the Lord shared with me, He was coming to take her home. He, Himself would come and she should take His hand and go with Him, not to worry about Phil. Phil is my dad. He will take care of him. I was surprised by this. I asked how I could know this was my Heavenly Father. He told me to call her and ask her this question. "How long have you known". He told me not to say anything till she answered. I called mom later that morning and asked her that question. "Mom, how long have you known." She responded with, "I do not know what you are talking about." I again asked the question, "Mom, how long have you known". She responded, "2 weeks." She said, "you heard from the Lord again?" She asked what I heard. I told her I would tell her what I heard in the Spirit after she told me what she knows.

She shared how the doctor told her she has two months to two years left to live. Her organs where failing. She was currently suffering with bronchitis. She passed a way three months later from heart, lung and kidney failure.

The day she passed I had an uneasy feeling in my spirit. At this time, my mom had been in a nursing facility for three days. I called to check up on her. When they answered the phone, I asked to speak to her. The person on the phone asked who I was and how I was related to Claire. I told them who I am and that I am her daughter. I was told to wait on the line. Another person got on the phone and asked again who I was and how I am related. I told that person the same thing as the first. I then said, "look I just want someone to go in her room if she can't come to the phone and tell her that I love her and everything is going to be ok. The second person then said wait one minute and put me on hold. I found this very odd. Now, a third person came on the phone and again asked who I was and how I am related. I told her the same as the others. I then repeated again, I just want someone to go in her room and tell her I love her and everything will be ok! The women informed me she was the charge nurse and my mother took her last breath while I was on the phone.

Wow God! How very faithful you are. He helped me walk my mother home those last few years. I called to say I love you and everything will be ok. I believe she heard that and she took Jesus's hand and went home.

Life is not always easy, sometimes our loved ones leave before we are ready to let them go. I so appreciated that God allowed the two of us to journey that time together, so when the time came, I could let go and release her into His hands. Mom was only 56 years old. Because of the Lord leading me, my greatest fear became my greatest honor and service to both God and my mom.

To all who have lost one of your most precious loved ones, I hope when you look back you will see His grace and love was with the both of you at that time and remains with you now. So sorry for your loss.

Revelation 21:4

'He will wipe every tear from their eyes. There will be no more death' or mourning or crying or pain, for the old order of things has passed aways.'

John 14:3 Jesus said:

'Let not your heart be troubled; you believe in God, believe also in me. In My Fathers house are many mansions; if it were not so, I would have told you. I go to prepare a place for you. And if I go prepare a place for you, I will come again and receive you to Myself; that where I am, there you may be also. And where I go you know, and the way you know.'

THE MAN OF MY DREAMS

JANET

In most girls' dreams, they want the perfect husband and children to love. I was no different. I always hoped for this. When time had passed and wounds were mended by God, I wanted that dream. I, however, wanted God's will for my life more. I had a desire to either marry and have another child, or when Jeremy finished school to sell everything and go into the mission field. I knew the best way to know His will would be to ask Him to show me what that was, and He did.

I had a dream one evening about a little girl with blonde curly hair and blue eyes. Her name was Anna Marie. In my dream, she did not seem to be my child but she was important to me. The dream was very real, unlike others. We were playing outside in a yard. I was not sure if the dream was of importance. I told God if He was trying to tell me something, I need more understanding as to what that was.

I then had another dream. In the dream Anna Marie and I were playing outside, and another little girl came and sat by me. This little girl had brown hair and brown eyes, she looked like me. Her name was Anna Clare. Anna Clare and Anna Marie were about two or three years apart in age. I knew this child was mine. In the dream we all played together and laughed together.

I had a third dream. In this dream it was Anna Clare and I in the backyard playing. Anna got up and ran around the side of the house. She was not running from me. She was running to someone. She was giggling and excited. She ran up to a tall dark-haired man getting something out of his white car. I was not able to see his face. I knew this man was my husband.

I shared my dream with a very dear friend, Denise. Denise and I spent a lot of time together. She had a son named Phil, he was the same age as Jeremy. We shared our hearts with each other as we journeyed through our 20's and 30's raising our own sons. We were both excited to see what God was going to do. Denise, at the time, had remarried and was expecting a child.

That August, Denise and Jim were blessed with a little baby girl. Anna Marie was here, blonde curly hair and blue eyes. God is so good. Then the realization hit if she was here, I would be meeting my husband soon in order for the timeline of the age of the girls to line up.

The next spring, I attended a funeral of the ex-husband of a friend of mine. I went to give my friend some moral support. I did not really know this man. This is where I met a man named Douglas. We talked the evening away sharing our stories and love for the LORD. He was unlike any other man I have ever met.

Doug and I became friends and hung out some. Denise came to town, and we met up with her so we could meet little Anna Marie. She was so beautiful. Denise kicked my shoe and whispered to me, "He drives a white car, remember the white car?" I thought oh my, he does drive a white car.

Doug and I hung out as friends and within a year, we got married. I truly married the man of my dreams. August 3, 1998, Anna Clare Hince was born. Anna had brown hair and blue eyes. When she was about 9 months old, I questioned God why her eyes were blue, because in my vision her eyes were brown. Overnight her eyes turned brown. Now my vision was complete. Anna Clare is three years younger than Anna Marie by one day.

This reminds me of the scripture Psalm 37:4 *Delight yourself in the Lord, and He will give you the desires of your heart. (English Standard Version)*

I so desired to have the family God intended for me. To be married to a man of God, who loved the LORD as much as I did. A man I could trust, pray with and more than that, serve the LORD with.

I was blessed with both of my desires. I married the man of my dreams, and we had a beautiful daughter together. I was blessed with a man who loved and helped raise my son Jeremy John as his own. I also was blessed with two stepsons, whom I love as my very own, Jeremy Joe and Jeff.

I have learned that wherever I am, as long as I am loving, caring and helping people for Christ it is the mission field I'm called to. I do not need to leave the country to do this. Wherever I am, He is. Wherever He is and places me is the mission field that I am called to. I am so very thankful and blessed.

THE DESIRE OF MY HEART

JANET

Psalm 37:4 reads, *"Delight yourself also in the Lord and He shall give you the desires of your heart."*

I had been walking in a relationship with the Lord for some time. I grew very close to Him. Jesus meant everything to me. I was growing in my walk with Him more and more each day. I had found for myself the greatness of His love, compassion and forgiveness for all people including myself. I was attending church, going to bible studies, reading the bible and fellowship with others who also turned to Jesus.

When I moved to St. Cloud my sister Joyce joined me a few months later. She left her abusive husband and wanted a better life for her daughter and herself. She like me went to counseling and made better choices for her future. Joyce and I shared an apartment together and help each other with our children. We became very close. I love my sister Joyce so very much.

She and I got our own apartments about a year later. She joined some support groups to help in her journey. I became closer and closer to the Lord. Joyce really struggled with my becoming what she called religious. I would share my new found treasure of Jesus. She did not want any thing to do with it. She had her Higher Power through her support groups and that was good enough.

We still did things together and hung out. She eventually met a man and they got married. I would share my faith with her and she would tall me not to talk to her about it. She was very adamant about it. On one occasion, she was talking about her Higher Power as she was driving us somewhere. I got up the boldness to ask her if her Higher Power was Jesus. She literally popped up and hit her head on the ceiling of the car. She snapped back at me and that was the end of the conversation.

Not to long after that while visiting in her living room, I started to share with her something God put on my heart. She stopped me and told me not to ever talk about Him again or she would have be to cut off our relationship. I was shocked. Then I started to cry and told her that to stop talking about Jesus would be to close off the most important part of who I am. I told her I could not do that. I shared a few more things with her, told her I love her and this is good bye then. She looked at me in disbelief.

I walked out of her home never to return.

About 3 weeks later I got a phone call from her. She said, "Are you serious, you do not intend to see me anymore." I told her she was the one who told me not to come back if I talk about Jesus.

Joyce and I then would get together. I would still share some of the cool things I was learning in the bible. She one day started to ask me a few questions and then would remark you have 5 minutes to answer. When you are learning about the work of God, it takes more than 5 minutes to answer. This went on in our visits for some time. Eventually the 5 minutes turned in to 10. She really could only handle those few minutes each time we got together. This went on for several months.

I was dating Doug and we decided to get married. I was so very excited. We took our commitment to the Lord very seriously and still do. I knew my maid of honor had to be a Christian who took their faith to heart, a believer. My hearts desire would be to have Joyce be my maid of honor. She at this point had not accepting Jesus into her heart. I went before the Lord and reminded Him of His promise to give me the desire of my heart because I delight in him. I told him I am not sure how He will do it but He has 3 months.

Joyce has a son Zac. She took him to a Fall Fun Fest in St. Cloud and Zac went forward to receive Jesus in his heart. When he did this, it made Joyce think more on this. She did give her life to the Lord before my wedding, she was my maid of honor. Praise God!

The amazing thing was I prayed for her salvation for 12 years and never gave up. She is an amazing Christian woman. I love my sister very much. I love sharing my faith with her and praying together for others. Never give up. God loves each and every person. He wants the very best for them just like we do. He is the very best!

ANNA'S TESTIMONY

Hi, my name is Anna. I am 23 years old and I am a Christian. I was raised in a Christian home. My parents taught me about Jesus my whole life. At six years old, I went to a vacation Bible Camp through Joy Christian Center and it was there when I asked Jesus into my heart, to be my LORD and Savior. I have experienced God being involved in my life in many ways and l have had a lot of answered prayers. As a matter of fact, I am an answer to prayer. My mother and I almost died during my birth into this world. There were people including my dad praying for my mom and me. I became deaf at 2 months, again my parents prayed for me, and I started hearing. I was diagnosed with Autism. My parents would not accept that diagnosis and prayed God's word over me for years. Mark 11:23-24 says, *"the things that you believe and pray for, you can have what you say and believe."* They also worked with me and supported me. The professionals took the diagnosis of Autism off me. I am now normal and doing well. My parents have taught me the word of God and the power of prayer. I read the Bible with my parents, I led many friends to know the LORD, and have seen God answer many prayers for my parents as well. I also see God in nature; I know this world didn't just happen by chance. In Romans 1 it talks about Gods invisible attributes are clearly seen through His creation of the earth. One example I would like to share with you today, is my heart of compassion towards others. In Romans Chapter 5 Verse 5 it says, *"God put His love in my heart and His love is compassion for the lost."* I would like to share a story with you of an experience I had with God's compassion to reach out to my friend Jenna. Jenna was born handicapped, with no muscles. She was restricted to many things, she couldn't walk at all, and she had a lung problem, that's just a few of the health problems she had to cope with. Her mother never took her to church, but we shared a half-brother which took her to church with him sometimes. Due to her many health problems, she did not have a very long-life expectancy and God started to move in my heart to share the message of Salvation with Jenna. So, my parents and I made a special road trip one weekend, to go visit Jenna up in Grand Rapids, MN. We went there with the purpose to share Jesus's plan of salvation with her. I explained it to her and after talking with her, I asked her if she would like to receive Jesus into her heart. My parents, our brother, and I all prayed the salvation prayer with her. A couple months later I heard the horrifying news that Jenna was no longer with us, but God reassured me that she was with Him and no longer in pain down here on earth. Being a Christian and knowing God is real, it brought me comfort and peace to accept it in the sadness of her passing. God has truly revealed Himself to me in many ways; that was just one of them. Jesus is an awesome Savior and He is called the author and finisher of our faith, Ephesians chapter 2 verses 8 – 9 says *"It's by his grace that we receive the gift of faith to be saved, to have confidence in our heart, that he is real and we will spend eternity with him."* In Philippians 1:6 it says, *"We can have confidence that Jesus started a good work in our heart and he will continue that good work until the day of his return."*

BROWN SHOES

JANET

I really think God has a sense of humor. I can remember a time in our marriage when things were tight. Every penny was accounted for, and the children's needs came before Doug and mine. Like many people, we can have times in our life where we pout, and that's exactly what I did. I had asked God if he would please somehow allow me to get a pair of brown shoes. I wanted them to wear with my outfits to church and other places. Every time paydays came, another need arose, and that money was spent elsewhere.

Some time had passed and still no brown shoes. On one particular day, I was visiting with a very close friend. I was having a pity party, sharing with my friend my frustration over not being able to get a pair of brown shoes. My friend's daughter overheard the conversation and came upstairs and said, "What size shoe do you wear?" I told her a size 9, thinking nothing of it, and continued with my conversation. She disappeared from the room to return with a brown pair of brand-new shoes that were the exact size and style that I wanted! She told me to try them on. To my amazement, they fit perfectly. She said she had bought them for a great price and that she was going to use them as slippers. She told me I could have them. The odd thing is this young lady only wears a size 6 shoe. She insisted not only that I have them, but that she would not take a dime for them. We all had a laugh and thanked God for His gift and reminder that He does hear our prayers and answers them in mysterious ways. On another note, this young lady became my daughter-in-law years later. She did not know my son at the time she gave me the shoes. God is so good, so very good!

Sometimes when the journey is long, and we need encouragement, God is so aware of it all. He finds ways to bless us despite our childish behaviors.

He knows the real issue for my pouting was not the brown shoes. I just needed to know He was there and that my need, no matter how small, was important to Him. His word says in 1 Peter 5:7 *casting all our care upon Him, for He cares for you.* I casted my care, but I did not give Him the time to come through. He came through in a way that so blessed me, as simple as through a young woman with a kind heart, who would one day become my daughter-in-law.

GOD CALLS A BURGER TIME OUT

JANET

On one of those beautiful summer weekends, we planned a trip up north to spend with Doug's family. We made the two-and-a-half hour journey many times. We usually stop on our way up for lunch or a snack.

This particular weekend was no different except when we got to Brainerd I wanted to stop at McDonald's for burgers. This was not one of our usual stopping places. I was not really hungry but felt the need to stop. I felt the need to stop now, not really knowing why. I sometimes get these strong urges; I call them warnings from God. So, after some insistence, Doug pulled into the McDonald's parking lot. The kids were glad to stop, as they enjoy burgers and fries, and Anna loved the playland.

We were sitting and eating our burgers maybe for a half an hour or so, when we saw and heard fire trucks, police cars and ambulances going by in the direction we were heading. I looked at Doug and wondered what had happened.

Doug and I gathered the kids when it was time to go. The boys were in their teens and our daughter was about two years old. When we got to the signal light and needed to go straight, a police officer waved us over and informed us the road was closed ahead, due to a very serious accident a few miles up the road. This meant we had to go the long way up north. Doug was not too happy, and neither was I. We looked at each other and wondered what had happened and when? We would have been going in that direction. We continued our way and ended up having a great weekend.

When we had gotten home from the weekend, we had heard that a family was hit head on by a car driven by a 16 year old boy trying to pass a car. The mother had been killed and some of the children were hurt in the collision. The vehicle that was hit, was the vehicle that was originally behind us on the way up north. I so grieve the loss of that family.

I believe God tries to warn us a lot of times or even tells us when to do things. I do not believe for one moment that that particular family's loss was God's plan. He loves them just as much as He loves me. I am saying that He does let us know things: like stop here, turn there or do not go. I have had things like this happen over and over in my life and I have learned to listen to the voice of God. Sometimes it is a still small voice, sometimes a feeling in the pit of your stomach or even just a knowing. God is always there for us. I really believe this to be true. I do hear His voice.

John 10:1-42 Talks about the sheep knowing the voice of God.

"... The sheep hear His voice, and He calls His own sheep by name and leads them out. When He has brought out all His own, He goes before them, and the sheep follow Him, for they know His voice. A Stanger they will not follow, but they will flee from him, for they do not know the voice of strangers."

Many of you hear His voice and recognize it; others hear Him and are not aware it is Him speaking to you. Others hear His voice and tune Him out. I encourage you to listen and obey; when He speaks it is always for your good, for He loves you more than you could ever know.

A RIDE TO SCHOOL

JANET

It started off as an ordinary day. Jeremy was now in High School getting ready to leave for school. Anna played in the other room as I was at the kitchen sink doing dishes. I heard a car pull up into the driveway. This was not uncommon for one of Jeremy's friends to pick him up. I did not recognize the car. As Jeremy rushes by me, I asked who was picking him up. He said," Billie," and out the door he went. Billie pulled out of our driveway and down the street really fast. I thought to myself Billie needs to slow down. I said a short prayer under my breath.

I continued working on the dishes. I started to get a sick feeling in the pit of my stomach, like something was horribly wrong. I felt a strong sense to pray for Jeremy. I sometimes get that need to pray for others. I felt a very strong need to pray for his protection, which did not make sense to me. The school was about a mile away. Jeremy surely would be at school by now. I started to pray for him, and the sense got stronger and stronger. I prayed as the Holy Spirit led me to pray.

About an hour after school started Jeremy called me. He said, "Mom, there was a car accident. I am okay."

I said, "You're funny! You're at school, you left over an hour ago. So, what do you really need?"

He said, "MOM, there was a car accident. Billie and I went out to Nemethe's to pick him up. We were going to be late for school, so Billie was driving fast. When we got on the gravel road close to his house, Billie lost control of the car. It went off the road and started to roll. It rolled over and over till it hit a tree and stopped. Billie was knocked unconscious, and her brother was thrown from the car."

I could not believe what I was hearing. Jeremy then said that he got out of the car and walked about a mile away to the nearest farm. They called for help. The ambulance driver wanted to take him to the hospital, but he did not want to go. The ambulance driver then talked to me. He said that Jeremy seems to look okay and that it was up to me whether he would be taking Jeremy to the hospital with the other two kids. I told the driver that the police officer could bring him home and I would take him to the doctor, which I did. Jeremy was fine and I was told to keep an eye on him. Billie had a concussion, and her brother suffered a broken arm.

That evening, Jeremy shared more about the roll over. He told me that he did not have his seat belt on. As they were rolling, he was tossed around and just before they hit the tree the upper part of his body was hanging out the door. Just as the car was about to crush his head and chest, the car hit the tree which stopped the car from crushing him. He would have died. My heart sank and then I remember the words "PRAY FOR JEREMY'S SAFTEY." WOW, GOD, WOW!!! I wished after the fact I would have prayed for Billie and her brother. Thankfully they turned out okay too.

One can wonder about events like this. How do we know when you hear from God? Sometimes it is a reading from the word, through the Bible, another person, a knowing in your heart or perhaps a still small voice. However you hear, or get an understanding of what He tells you, listen and act on it. That day it was both knowing something was wrong and a still small voice. Prayer was all that was needed to save my son's life at that moment. He told me what to pray and I did.

He knows, He listens, and He will show or tell you what to do. Listen, just listen and trust. He knows. He knows and cares for you and your loved ones. He Knows! Psalm 121:8 *The Lord will watch over your coming and going both now and forevermore.*

GOD PROVIDED BEFORE THE NEED AROSE

DOUG

This story is about how God used a Christian radio station to answer my prayer.

As a Christian, I was praying and believing God for help in every area of my life.

The financial area of my life needed a lot of help from God.

I went through a divorce and was paying child support among all the other obligations of life. This included rent, food, car, taxes; you know, everyday life expenses.

Money was very tight. There never seemed to be any extra, but God was always helping me work it out.

In this incident, I was driving my car on the highway and hit a piece of wood on the road, causing my tire to go flat. I then pulled over and changed the tire.

Looking at both the tire and wheel then seeing the damage done from the wood, it was obvious I would need to buy a new tire and a new wheel.

I put my spare tire on and drove home.

Nothing ever takes God by surprise. He is all knowing, all powerful, and all present.

God knew I was going to have this problem come about and He provided for me before the problem even came to be.

Now I will tell you the rest of the story: how God used my sister and the Christian radio station to help me.

You see, God uses people, places, and things to answer our prayers.

He allows us to be part of what He is doing in people's lives.

The Christian radio station had just come to St. Cloud and as a way to promote the station, they allowed anybody to call in a person's name to go into a drawing to win 100 dollars. If that name was drawn, they would announce it on air and that person had to call in to the radio station within 15 minutes to win.

My sister called my name into the contest and the Radio station drew my name and announced it, I called in and won the 100 dollars.

I picked the money up that day after work and about ten minutes afterwards is when I had the tire problem.

At first, I was upset about the tire, and I was complaining, you know, giving voice to my frustration. I was saying, "that figures I win 100 dollars and now it's going to cost me 100 dollars for a tire and used rim."

God spoke to my heart and said I knew this problem was going to happen and I provided for you before the need arose.   WOW, God is so good!

I encourage you to read Psalm 139. The Bible says God knows everything about us.

God says He knows every thought we have, everything that will happen in our life, good and bad. (side note} God's not the one causing the bad things in people's lives. We have a free will, capable of making choices, both good and bad. We live in a sinful, fallen world. People's choices affect things.

The good news is, God loves us and wants to help us in our lives. If we love God and trust Him with our lives, He will work things out for our good! He will provide for us. He promises this to us and I believe

Him at His word. Sometimes God will provide the answer to our problem before there is a problem.

BOB AND ESTHER – GOD'S GOODNESS

JANET

I have discovered that God will go to great lengths to save a soul that is lost. This story began in a small town of Royalton where my husband and I owned a home. We lived there for about five years. Then, the LORD put it on my heart to prepare for a move. In a heart-to-heart talk with God, I told him that He had better share that with Doug. I did not think Doug would agree with it. About three weeks later, Doug came home from work and said, "I think we are supposed to the sell the house." I informed him that I got that three weeks ago in prayer. He said, "why didn't you tell me?" I said, "I did not think you would be open to it unless you got it from God."

We prayed and asked God where He wanted us to move to. God does not always tell us the where, when, and how's in life. Most of the time you must go with the peace of your heart. The peace in your heart is the leading of the Holy Spirit. If you have total peace, you can trust your decision. If you have no peace, wait or keep looking. Philippians 4:6-7 says, *do not be anxious about anything, but everything by prayer and supplication with thanksgiving let your requests be made known to God. The peace of God, which surpasses all understanding, will guard your heart and minds in Christ Jesus.*

We looked at a house and got no peace. We looked at a mobile home and got no peace. We looked at different towns, and no peace. We decided to look at apartments in different towns and got no peace. Then we both decided to look at apartments where I used to live in Sartell, before Doug and I were married. As we drove up to the apartments, Doug told me the only way he would move into one of the units was if we could have a ground floor walk out. He pointed at his first and second choice. We met with the management moments later to look at units that were open. There were no ground floor walk outs available. We both thought, "now what?"

Within a few days, the manager called and informed us there was a unit available on the ground floor. He mentioned someone had put in their notice. We went to look at the apartment. Guess what? Yes, you got it! It was Doug's first choice. The kitchen floor looked a little rough. I asked if they could replace it. The manager said, "not at this time, but maybe later." Doug and I both knew for whatever reason this would be home for a while. When we moved into the unit, they had replaced not only the kitchen floor, but the carpets too. God is so good!

We had not lived there for long when we met this very cute elderly couple, Bob and Esther. Bob was 94 years old, and his spunky wife Esther was 99 years old. They were very sharp in their mind and able-bodied people. They were healthy, able to walk, and even dance. We became very close friends and adopted them into our family. For the next few years, we took them places, visited on our front patio and listened to their wonderful stories of the past. One of our favorite things was to take the couple to McDonald's for an ice cream cone, in which Esther would eat the cone and Bob would eat the tip of the cone. She would put the ice cream in a cup for Bob. We enjoyed sharing our faith with them and talking about the love God had for them. We told them he would take care for them and watch over them. God will bring people in their path when they have a need.

Two years or so after we met the wonderful couple, Bob's cancer had become worse. He was placed in a nursing home nearby. Doug and I would take Esther to visit him and sometimes we would visit him on our own time. On a visit when Doug went by himself, Bob told him it will all be over soon. Doug promised Bob that we would watch over Esther and take good care of her. He said, I am counting on it."

We kept our promise to Bob. We took Esther everywhere we went. We helped her with tasks she could no longer do. We loved our little Bob and Esther. Esther lived to be 107 years old.

The day Esther went home to be with Bob, I was painting my deck. I felt a strong prompting from the LORD to go pick her up for dinner at our house. I fought the urge, but finally gave in. I called her and she did not answer. I drove over to her apartment, as Doug and I bought a house a few months back. I asked her if she would like to come for a meal. She said, "I have heartburn, I am not hungry, but I will come for the company." Later that evening after supper and a drive to Menards, I took her home. For the first time, she needed help. I helped her dress for bed. I wanted to take her to the Emergency Room, but she refused. I told her to call the doctor in the morning and I would take her in. She agreed. She promised to call me if she got worse. She called me later that night. We called an ambulance, then I drove over to her apartment. When the ambulance arrived, I drove to meet her at the Emergency Room. Esther had a heart attack. She passed away that night and

I was with her the entire time. God is so very good. Just a few days before she passed away, in a time of prayer, I asked the LORD if I could be there with her when it was her time to go. I loved her so very much and I did not want her to be alone when her time came. He granted my request.

I really believe God will ask you to do things that do not make sense in this world. Why would he ask us to sell our home? Why would he want us to go into an apartment? Why would we get the first-choice apartment? He knew there was a special elderly couple, who would need a touch from him and a helping hand from God, their father. Bob and Esther did not know the true love of Jesus until God showed up through two obedient servants willing and desiring to serve God and love man.

BEN

JANET

Doug and I lived in an apartment for a while when Anna was a little girl. She often begged us for a dog. The apartment we lived in at the time had a "no pets" policy. We told her when we moved into a house one day that she could get a dog.

While we were house hunting, I asked a friend of mine by the name of Jackie what type of dog she would recommend for Anna. She owned a dog boarding place and knew quite a bit about dogs. Jackie said, "A shiatsu would be a good fit for her". One day Jackie called me and told me that one of her clients had a 6-month-old Shiatsu puppy they wanted to find a home for. We did not own a home yet. Jackie said, "If you would like the dog, I will board him for free until you find yourselves a home." At the time, we were in the midst of house hunting. We were so excited as we drove to Jackie's to meet this little dog. We fell in love with this adorable black and white pup. We sought to buy him.

Jackie called a few days later and told us the people decided to keep him. Anna was devastated. I shared with her that if this puppy was not meant to be ours that God had another one meant for her. We prayed as she cried and placed it in God's hands.

She was so sad. There was nothing we could do. My friend said she would keep an eye out for another dog.

About a month later we moved into our new home. We were so happy to be in our house finally. Jackie called a day or so later and said the family with Ben changed their mind again. She wanted to know if we were still interested! I told her we would love to take Ben.

We moved into our house and got Ben in April. It was also my birthday in April. I planned for Ben to be brought to our house after Anna got off the bus one day. I told her that Jill was coming over after school to drop off my birthday present. She thought Jill was someone I worked with. When Jill showed up with Ben, Anna was confused. Who is this lady? It was not the Jill she knows. What is this lady doing with a puppy? Then she recognized it was Ben and she went crazy. I said, "Yes Ben is here to stay".

I was so happy that God blessed us with this puppy. We prayed and trusted Him to bring Ben to us or bless us with another puppy. I find when I trust God it always works out.

H O U S E
P R O V I S I O N

DOUG

This story is about God answering our prayer to purchase a home.

When my wife and I got married, we were able to purchase a small, older home and we were grateful God blessed us to do so.

We stayed in our first home for about five years and then we decided to sell. We rented for another five years to get our finances in a better spot.

As Christians, my wife and I prayed all the time about our life. We asked God to guide us according to His will and plan.

We rented a very nice, cozy walkout apartment. We both were content and believed we were where God wanted us for that season of time, which we weren't sure just how long it was going to be when we first moved there.

After about five years, we were both feeling we needed a change. We had a desire to purchase another home, but we weren't sure how we would be able to afford one.

Our finances were in an okay spot for the cost of renting but buying a home would be a significant increase in our budget.

On paper looking at our income and calculating the extra expenses that owning a home would be, it didn't look very promising. However, we know God is able to make a way when there doesn't seem to be one. The Bible says all things are possible to him who believes.

Jan said, "Let's just go online and see what the market is looking like". We were kind of dreaming and looking to see what houses were selling for.

We talked about what we would want in a house, and we were being very specific about it.

Our Heavenly Father is into details, He invites us to pray specifically what we are asking Him for.

We prayed and asked God to guide us to a house with the things we were wanting and if it is His will that we buy a house now.

We went to some open houses that realtors were having and started moving forward in the process of purchasing a home.

It was a step of faith to even look because we didn't have any money for a down payment.

One day, Jan and I were praying about buying a home and we said let's sow a financial seed, an offering to a ministry and believe God for money for a down payment.

Not that you can buy God's blessings, but the word of God says there are spiritual laws that God put in place when He created the world.

One of those laws says, *give and it will be given back to you, good measure, pressed down, shaken together, your cup shall run over.*

Another law says, *what you sow you shall reap, and God is able to multiply what you give so more comes back to you.*

Another law says *seek God and His righteousness and His kingdom first and He will add the blessings of life to you.*

These verses are found in Luke 6, 2 Corinthians 9, and Matthew 6.

We made a vow to God to give a $1000 offering to a ministry. We didn't have it at the time, but we said we would make payments as the money came in. God knew our heart that we would make good on the promise. In faith we bought a food and water dish for the dog we believed we would get when we purchased a home.

We prayed and said, "God we are believing you for money towards the down payment of our house if it is according to your will at this time."

We had peace in our heart that it was okay, so we moved forward and continued to go to open houses.

One time we were at an open house, and I overheard the realtor telling someone about a $8,000 grant if you haven't owned a home in the past three years.

I asked the realtor, "what was that all about?"

He said, "the government is giving a $8,000 grant to anyone who hasn't owned a home in the past three years."

We sold our first home five years ago.

We checked into it more and we qualified for it, but you don't get the money until next year on your taxes. Basically, we would need it now for the down payment, not buy a house and then get reimbursed a year later.

Once again, we prayed and asked God for favor, for wisdom what to do.

God uses people, places and things to answer your prayers.

God put on our heart to ask my mom if she could lend us the money and we would pay her back next year. She did, and it was a huge blessing for her to help us.

We also had to consolidate a couple financial obligations into one smaller loan so we could afford the new house payment. We knew it was a temporary issue and we would pay it off shortly.

The bank said no at first, but I don't give up easily, I believed it was a test of our faith. I asked the small bank branch first, then the main bank next. They both said no, so we prayed and said, "God we ask for favor," then went back to the first bank and asked again. This time they said yes, as long as we had a co-signer. My brother in-law helped us.

Wow, it was coming together! We were excited.

We went to some more open houses to find a house with our very specific list and the realtor told us there was about ten homes that would be close to what we wanted and could afford.

We wanted a house ten years or newer in Sartell, a spare bedroom for company, an extra room for Jan's crafts, maintenance free siding, and windows. The roof had to be good, and we also wanted a walk-in closet and also a nice yard to get a dog for Anna.

God is so amazing! He led us to a house that fit our detailed list perfect and $10,000 under appraisal price, WOW.

Turns out the back yard even had a white maintenance free fence for the dog which we did get for our daughter.

We moved in about a year after we started the process of faith and dreaming and praying about buying a house.

The month we moved in we made our last $100 payment to the ministry that we vowed to God. Coincidence? I think not. I know the hand of God was all over this process. God answered our prayers!!!!!

GOD PROVIDES VACATION MONEY

DOUG

God cares about every area of our lives. Yes, even vacations.

This story is about a summer vacation my wife and I were planning.

We were making plans to go on a 5-day motorcycle trip on the north shore of Duluth, MN.

We are people who live on a budget. We budget each month for our regular bills and anything extra we know that is coming due.

It was June, and we were getting ready for our motorcycle trip in a couple weeks. We had budgeted for the gas, hotels, spending money, food, etc.

One area we didn't have covered for was Jan's missing wages for her job the week we were going to be gone. We didn't overlook it, we just didn't have the extra money to replace the wages.

She works two part time jobs; one job has paid vacation and the other one doesn't.

We were needing 200 dollars more. We knew God would help us; we just weren't sure how He was going to do it.

As Christians, we pray about every area of our lives and invite God to be with us. Yes, and that even means vacations.

It was a beautiful summer morning; Jan and I were having coffee on our deck and we were talking about the trip we were going on in a few weeks.

We were reading the Bible, and we were praising God for His goodness.

We prayed about the 200 dollars we still needed and God spoke to Janet's heart and said, "Do you trust me?"

She said, "yes, LORD, we do."

We finished our coffee and prayer time, then we went for a motorcycle ride just for the day, no set route to go on, just random picking roads in the country.

I told Janet, "Maybe we should ride over to A&W and have a root beer and sandwich." So, that's what we did.

Well, we were about to experience a set up by perfect

timing from God.

You see, God knows everything and can guide you to be in the right place at the right time.

God led us to go there at just the right time, there was a radio station there and they were having a drawing to win two weekend passes to the WeFest concert, which had a 400 dollar value.

Right after we were done eating, they were going to do the drawing and Janet asked, "what is the drawing for?" We didn't have a clue what it was for, but they told us and Janet put her name and my name in the box. They shook up the box and drew a name but it wasn't ours. We said, "Oh well, let's go."

I said, "I have to use the bathroom then we can go." Meanwhile, the name they drew didn't have a phone number on it so it was not counted valid, so they drew another name and it was mine. Praise God!

I came out of the bathroom and the radio guy says, "high five Doug my man, you won the tickets!"

I said, "what? I thought Tyler won."

He said, "No phone number on the ticket, so we had to redraw and you won!"

Wow, I thought awesome, but we don't go to WeFest

concerts. Of course, I didn't tell him that, I said, "cool, thanks a lot."

Then my lightning-fast mind thought we will sell them for a discounted price and use the money for vacation.

God provides in many ways, don't ever try to figure it out.

The Bible says to honor God, put Him first place in our lives and we try to do our best to trust and obey Him.

We tithe of our income and believe God at His word. His word says if you honor Him, He will honor us and provide for us! We believe it and have seen it work in our lives time and time again, GOD IS FAITHFUL!

SORES NO MORE

JANET

I have learned a lot about the power of prayer, standing on the word of God and believing God at His word. I have seen this work in my life and in others' lives.

I used to work in a restaurant called Twin Pines outside of a town called Rice. I was a waitress, and it was a place God called me to minister to others. I saw so many miracles come to pass there in the lives of the people passing through.

One morning the LORD brought this elderly man into the restaurant. He was very kind. I noticed he had gauze bandages all over his arm. I was very curious about the wounds that seemed to be seeping through the bandages. I also noticed he was careful how he moved them and set his arms down.

I said, "Your arms look painful."

He said, "It is very painful. I have some kind of illness that is causing my body to eat my skin. The sores are to the bone. The doctors are not sure what to do." He looked hopeless and shrugged his shoulders.

I returned to work. I started to pray for him as I was waiting on other tables. I felt a tugging on my heart and a drawing to go back to the man's table. I asked him if he believed in Jesus. He said yes, that he was asking Him to heal him. I asked the man if I could pray with him. He said, "Please do, I would really like that."

I prayed the scripture: *By his stripes, we are healed.* This is found in 1Peter 2:24. I also prayed *No weapon formed against you shall prosper,* found in Isaiah 54:17. We talked about the fact that Jesus loves him and wants him to receive his healing.

He finished his meal and thanked me for the encouraging word and prayer. With a hand wave he left the restaurant.

About six months later, a very happy and kind man walked in the restaurant. This man said, "Hi Jan good to see you." This happened a lot. People come and go. I do not always recognize them. He said, "Do you remember me." I smiled. He rolled up the arms of his shirt and said, "Not even a scar, Jan. Not even a scar." I knew right away who he was. He said the doctors could not explain how the wound began to heal, and the illness died off.

He gave me a hug and ordered some food. We chatted

and he was off to enjoy his life, healed completely of the flesh-eating illness. PRAISE BE TO GOD AND TO GOD ONLY!!!

D O U G ' S
S H O U L D E R
I N J U R Y

D O U G

In 2011, I needed shoulder surgery to repair two torn rotator cuff muscles.

In this story, you will see how God helped my wife and I with our finances. It really is an amazing testimony.

In the Bible, there is a scripture, Romans 8:28 that says *We know that all things work together for the good to those who love God, who are called according to His purpose.*

I love God and I know He has called me to live according to His purpose.

In life, we all will -- at some time -- experience bad situations and troubles that can rock your world.

Ironically, my wife also required shoulder surgery just six weeks before my injury occurred.

To tell this story and the miracles that took place, I should back up about a year before my injury took place and tell you something amazing that happened.

God spoke to my wife in a dream one night and she shared the message with me the next day. She said that God told her that He was going to give us a $100,000, which totally caught me off guard.

My mind couldn't grasp it at first, but I knew she didn't just make that up for something to say.

I thought, "how is that ever going to happen?" I didn't have a clue.

I said, "What, do you go to your mailbox one day and there is a check for a $100,000?"

A year after the dream, my wife needed that shoulder replacement surgery. She was going to be off work for a while, and we were trusting God to help us with our finances.

Six weeks after her surgery, I had my accident. I rescued our two little dogs from being attacked by a neighbor's dog at my father in-law's house.

In the process of wresting the boxer dog off my dogs, I tore two rotator cuff muscles. They were ripped away from the bone. They needed to be surgically reattached.

The surgeon said, "This is no small injury. You are in for a long road of recovery, and you'll be off work for nine months to heal up completely."

I thought, "Oh no! We are going to lose our house and everything we've ever worked for!" We didn't have savings to cover that kind of expense.

My wife helped me stay in faith. It was a challenge at first, as fear was trying to grip me.

We pray about everything good and bad; we want God involved in our lives.

We prayed and asked God for wisdom on what to do. God put on my heart a Bible verse in the book of Ecclesiastes, it says *if you wait for perfect conditions, you will never get anything done.*

I agreed, but at first, I thought, "How is that going to pay our bills or help us?"

This is where faith comes in. In the natural way of thinking, this next part won't make sense, because God's ways are not the same as man's ways.

God spoke to our hearts and said, "I want you to trust me and do what I say." He told us to sow a financial seed of $3,000 to a ministry.

God's word says, *give and it will be given back to you good measure, pressed down, shaken together and running over – will be poured into your lap. For with the measure you use, it will be measured back to you.* Luke 6:38.

At first, I wanted to tell God, "Don't you know we don't have any money?" (As if God didn't already know that.)

We were about to experience a miracle in our situation. We made a vow to pay it and we were totally committed. We would make payments or whatever it took to make it good. God knew our hearts.

We prayed and asked God for favor. I called the insurance company for the dog owner's home insurance.

I said, "The dog caused my injury and you are liable for my medical bills and lost wages." To my surprise, he didn't argue and started paying me every two weeks until I got back to work.

Wow God! You totally gave us favor! Insurance companies are not usually quick to pay without court or making you wait several months.

By law, my reimbursement wages were non-taxable that means I was taking home my gross pay, which covered our bills, and we were able to pay the $3,000 pledge.

The nine months of tax-free wages covered my wife's wages as well for the time she was off work.

WOW GOD!

Talk about an answered prayer! God moved in the insurance company's heart to give us favor; to pay all the medical bills and not to have to wait and go to court or delay wage reimbursement. Also, the punch line favor is they gave us a check for a $100,000 for pain and suffering.

Just like the dream God told my wife, that we were going to get a check for a $100,000!

It took faith to pray and believe that God had it under control. I never could have imagined this whole experience would have taken place.

God always works things out for the good to those who love and trust Him.

PROFIT SHARING MONEY RELEASED

DOUG

This story is about God giving me favor again as a result of praying, asking, and believing.

The Bible says all things are possible to Him who believes.

I want to point out something about prayer; not that I have it all figured out, but something I have learned.

When we pray, we must believe that what we are asking for is something we will receive, and later, we will receive.

Mark 11:24 says *when you pray, believe that you receive, and you shall have what you pray for.*

Notice the present tense when you pray, believe, and the future tense you shall have.

As believers in the Lord, we must believe before we see and then we will see it. Unbelievers say, "show me it first then I will believe it." That's backwards and not how prayer works.

One more thing about prayer is that it is according to God's timing, not ours.

Now for the story about profit sharing money from a place I used to work at:

I worked at place where part of our pay was profit sharing at the end of the year. We would get a statement showing us money the company added to our retirement, if they had a good year or not.

Some years were better than others, sometimes we didn't get any money and others we would get several thousand.

I worked at this company for 23 years.

It was a very stressful job. It paid well, but I was getting burned out at work.

I needed a change but really wasn't sure what my options were. God was about to change up my direction of life radically.

As a Christian I had a hunger to learn more about God and what life is all about.

Both my wife and I had a desire to go to Bible College, but never knew how it would be possible financially and still pay our monthly bills.

We talked about going to school a lot and how I

was needing a change from work. My work was affecting my health, it was very stressful.

One day we said, "lets step out in faith and go to school." God was leading us to trust Him, and He will guide us and He will provide us with new opportunities.

I didn't know how it was all going to work out, but we believed it would.

I thought I would work somewhere else but didn't have a place lined up yet. We stepped out in faith as God was challenging us to trust His plan. In the natural it was scary, not knowing how it was going to work.

I had 83-thousand dollars in my profit-sharing account at work, but it had stipulations on it.

The money was for retirement, and at the time I was only 50 years old, not ready to retire yet.

I had asked my boss several times in previous years if I could get the money, to which he always said no, I didn't qualify until I retired.

I had to quit and wait a minimum of two years to get the money, or reach the age of retirement, which I was only 50, so I didn't qualify yet.

In faith I gave my two weeks' notice and we signed up for two years of Bible College.

WOW, we were walking on water so to speak, God had to show up or we were in trouble.

After I gave notice of leaving work, which I was committed to, my wife and I were talking about how God has answered our prayers in other situations, and we believed He would help us again.

As I stated earlier that I asked several times to receive my profit-sharing money and was ALWAYS told NO!

We prayed and asked God for favor to move in my boss's heart and release the money.

We believed when we prayed. Then in faith a couple days later I asked Him for the money. It was a test of my faith.

WOW! talk about amazing to see firsthand the Spirit of God working right before my eyes.

When I asked my soon-to-be former boss if I could have my profit-sharing money, he first said, "Doug that is your retirement money."

I said, "I understand, but my wife and I could really use it now so we can go to bible school."

He hesitated for a few seconds, then God moved in his heart and he said, "okay, I will get you the papers and you can have your money in a couple weeks."

PRAISE GOD! God totally answered our prayer.

DISNEY TRIP
ANNA PRAYED
DOUG

This story is about an answer to prayer that our daughter Anna prayed.

In 2011, I was off work due to shoulder surgery. I was off work for several months to heal.

It was wintertime when this story took place, it was right after Christmas.

You know how winter can be challenging a lot of times. You are stuck inside the house due to cold weather and it can be boring.

Our daughter Anna was 13 at the time. She was off from school for a couple of weeks for Christmas break.

One night, my wife and I were sitting on the couch talking. Anna had already gone to bed, so she wasn't part of the conversation. She didn't have a clue we were talking about a vacation.

I said to Janet, "I'm bored we need to go somewhere on vacation!" I suggested out west because I love the mountains.

She said, "let's go somewhere warm instead."

She suggested Florida, to which it hadn't even entered my mind before the suggestion. I said, where in Florida?"

Janet said, "we should go to Disney World." I was shocked at first, I never thought about going to Disney World, I didn't see that one coming at all.

We talked more about it, and we planned more details about the trip. We decided to also go to Kennedy space station, NASA, Sea World, and the Holy Land experience in Orlando.

We were excited to go. We said let's do it! I couldn't wait to tell Anna the next day.

Before we told her the next day, I was surprised just how it happened. I was ready to tell her the exciting news, but God put on my heart to ask her first if she has prayed for anything specifically lately.

Anna was raised in a Christian home so it was common practice to pray about things often, such as protection, provision, hearts desires, and giving thanks.

I had no idea what she had been praying to God during her alone time with God, but God was about to show me that He hears and answers our prayers.

Like I said, I asked her if she prayed about anything specifically lately.

She said, "what do you mean?"

She wanted me to tell her something, and I explained, "I'm asking you, have you prayed lately?"

She got a smile on her face and said, "well, last night, I asked God if we could go to Disney World."

I was beside myself with shock, I couldn't believe it! I thought WOW God, then I told her that God definitely heard her prayer.

I said, "just last night Mom and I were talking about going on vacation and God must have spoken to mom's heart because we decided we are taking you to Disney World on vacation."

We had no idea Anna had prayed that very night and asked God for the trip to Disney World.

WOW! Talk about answered prayer! I'm still shocked how God first put on my heart to ask her first before we told her.

God was showing us He wants to bless us and answer our prayers, to give us desires of our heart.

I'm not saying that everything we ask for, we will always get, but God has answered so many of our prayers exactly what we asked for.

The Bible says it's the Fathers good pleasure to give good gifts to His Children. Luke 12:32

God is a good God, that's my story and I'm sticking to it!

LISTEN AND OBEY

JANET

This is a short but important story. I often spend time talking with God as I drive in my car. I really enjoy just sharing with Him, not always praying for someone or something, just talking and listening.

As I was going uptown on several occasions, I would see this sign on the side of the road, "A Home for The Day." It was an adult day care center located in a church not too far from my home. I did not pay a lot of attention to it, but enough that I noticed it. One day as I was passing the center, I was talking with the LORD, and I felt led to stop into the center. I was not sure why. I decided to go with the leading of the LORD. I was nervous and felt a little awkward as what to say. I pulled into the parking lot and went into the center.

I meet Betty, the person who owned and operated the center. She is a very kind and loving person. When I explained I was feeling lead by the LORD to stop in and chat with her, she was open and friendly. She too is a Christian, and we had a nice visit. I do not remember the initial conversation other than I shared my faith with her and she shared some of her thoughts with me. It was a warm and friendly visit. We both felt encouraged and lifted up. We exchanged phone numbers and I was on my way.

Some time had passed, then I received a call from Betty asking me if I would have some time to meet with her and possibly work for her part time. I took a resume in, and she interviewed me for a fill-in position as needed. I worked for Betty for a season before I started attending Charis Bible College. Working in the center was very rewarding, pouring love and grace into the lives of others, to build up and encourage the seniors. This is a beautiful thing. I loved the work I was called to do there, and the family I gained.

The workload of school and the center became too much, so I had to leave the center with much sorrow.

Proverbs 3:5-6 says: Trust in the Lord with all Your heart and lean not on your own understanding; In all your ways acknowledge Him, and He shall direct your path. As you share with Him and listen, He will direct the way He wants you to go. You can trust when He gives direction it will be the right way to go.

I would encourage everyone to listen and obey. God

knows what is best for us and others. Sometimes the mission is to help you or to help someone else. Life is a journey to be traveled with God and to share with others. His leading will bring many blessings, and life lessons in the journey ahead. Step by step, He leads, teaches and guides us to fulfill His plan for our life here on earth. May your journey be full of the awareness of His blessings.

GOD SENT MONEY TO OUR MAILBOX

DOUG

I will talk about three different times when God sent us money in our mailbox.

First of all, I need to clarify God is not a counterfeit, nor a thief, He is truth and never breaks it, He is Holy!

God uses people, places, and things to answer our prayers. He can do supernatural things, but usually will allow people to be part of the answer to your prayers.

He wants to do life with us, not just Him calling all the shots, so to speak.

We, as children of God, are part of His family and families interact with each other.

First story, my wife and I give to God's kingdom and what He is doing to help people. We give to the church and other people or wherever God is leading us to.

The Bible says to put God first place in our lives and

to honor Him in every area of our lives.

A few years ago, my wife and I were going through a challenging financial time; money was tight.

We trust God to help us in good times, hard times, and in between times.

Mathew 6:33 says *seek first the kingdom of God and His righteousness and He will add the things of life to us.*

We were praying and asking God for help in our finances. We needed Him to come through for us, He did!!!!! He is faithful.

We received a medium-sized manila envelope in the mailbox and we looked at the return address and it said Jehovah Jireh.

God refers to Himself in the Bible many ways. He uses different names to tell us about His character. Jehovah Jireh means "God our provider."

We have seen that and knew what that name meant. We opened the envelope and there was a $1,000 cash in it! We thought WOW GOD!

God put it on someone's heart to send us money which we were praying for. You see, God uses people to answer prayers.

The second story: when we first got married, finances were a struggle for us but by the Grace of God, we made it through.

One particular time, we were needing to buy groceries but we didn't have any money after paying our bills that week. However, we believed God would help us and He did.

We received $75 in cash in the mailbox. It had no return address on the envelope, and we knew it was God providing for us once again.

The third story: I was helping a ministry take care of some guys who just got out of prison or jail. The guys usually don't have any money when they first get out.

We helped them get housing and find a job. We were also helping them adjust back into society.

You see, we all make mistakes in life, just some are more severe. A lot of times, prison is a wakeup call and people serve their time and are sorry for what they did and need a second chance at life.

We don't judge them; we were trying to help them.

One guy had just got out of prison and he didn't have anything: no money, nothing to his name. He needed so much, but you can't do everything for them all at once.

I wanted to help him get a bicycle. I got a used one for him but it needed some work. It was going to be fifty dollars to get the bike and fix it, but all I had was fifty dollars, and at the time I needed it for my own needs. However, in faith, I gave it anyways and I trusted God would help me.

The next day I got a check in the mailbox for fifty dollars from a company I worked at about three years ago. I didn't have a clue they were sending me a check they owed me.

You see God says *give and it will be given back to you.* Luke 6:38 in the Bible.

I encourage you to always trust God and seek Him wholeheartedly, He will see you through!!!

GOD MAKES FAITH A PIECE OF CAKE

DOUG

This story is about God challenging me to step out in faith to buy a large amount of Dessert for a fund-raising event.

I will describe what happened. There was a Ministry putting on an event to raise money for the homeless.

The event had a large variety of soups for people to enjoy. You would pay a certain dollar amount and eat all you wanted.

The soups were donated by some local Restaurants. Several hundred people were expected to show up; it was a large event.

The Ministry putting on the event would supply the soups and desserts. There were people playing music and quilts being sold that some people donated. Overall, it was a fun time.

Here is where the story gets interesting: The day before the event, we were setting up tables and places for the music to be played, getting everything prepared for the next day.

The Pastor leading the fund-raising event called all of us workers together after we had everything set up for the next day.

The Pastor thanked us all for helping and was excited for the next day.

Then the Pastor told us some challenging news. She went on to explain that in the busyness of preparing for the large event somehow, she totally forgot to order dessert, which was a big thing to forget.

We prayed God would somehow work it out.

The Restaurants donated the soups, but the Ministry was needing to purchase the cake for dessert.

The pastor said there wasn't any money to purchase the large amount of cake needed. It should also have been ordered a few days in advance.

We prayed and believed God would work it out.

That's when the Spirit of God spoke to my heart and said, "what are you going to do about it?"

At first I told God, "what can I do?" I was looking at the problem from the natural viewpoint.

That's when God challenged me and said He wanted me to step out in faith and order the dessert.

I knew in my heart God would make it happen, but I didn't know how because I didn't have $200-$300 to buy the dessert.

In faith and obedience, I stepped out in faith and called the Bakery. I told them the situation and asked if they could make several large sheet cakes.

They asked, "when do you need them?" To which I responded by telling them that I needed them by the next morning. LOL!

I prayed before I called and asked God for favor. The Baker said they would see if they had enough ingredients to make them, which they did. I also asked if they would donate one cake, and they did.

God's hand was all over this task. I was a little nervous after I hung up the phone placing the order, but God was helping me to stay in faith.

I told God, "Well God you only got hours to raise the money, what should I do?"

I started calling people I knew – other Christians - and I asked if they would donate to the situation.

Within a couple hours, we raised the money. PRAISE GOD!

We not only raised enough money for the dessert,

but $60 extra and we were able to give to the fund raiser event to help the homeless.

I will admit, I was nervous ordering the dessert because I didn't have the money when I placed the order, but I had faith which God used to meet the need!

So, like the title says, God turned faith into cake!

SOWING AND REAPING TIME TOGETHER

DOUG

This story is a perfect example of a Bible verse in the book of Amos 9:13.

The verse talks about a time coming when the LORD will change up the gap of time between sowing a seed and reaping from the seed. They will happen at the same time.

Natural laws of planting seeds are that you put a seed in the ground and then you must wait a given amount of time before the seed grows and produces a harvest.

The LORD is truly the LORD of creation, and He controls time. After all, He created time and everything in the universe.

I read the verse before and heard others preach about it, but never did I really think I would experience it in my life.

It happened to my wife and I around the year 2015. I don't remember the exact date, but it was close to

2015.

My wife and I went to two years of Bible college. After graduating, we were holding a small bible study group once a week. We had about 10-15 people coming.

Sometimes people gave an offering to us, we weren't sure if we were going to start a church with the money we were getting. It wasn't a lot of money, but it was a start.

We had a single guy coming to our group and he loved God and wanted God's will for his life.

We taught a lot of different topics of the Bible. Sometimes money would come up as a group topic. The Bible has a lot to say about giving of our time, talent and treasure.

We have seen in the Word of God, that God talks about tithing of our income and the group agreed on the teaching Jesus said about money.

There was a particular single guy who was struggling some in his finances. He was coming to our group. As we know, it is a lot harder to make ends meet on one income rather than two.

My wife and I live on a budget. We tithe of our income and try to give above the ten percent when we can, not because we must, but because we want to be a blessing to others.

Here is where the story gets cool: God totally did a miracle with us and this single guy.

I'm not using his name because I haven't seen him lately to ask for permission to use his name, so I will just tell the story.

One day my wife and I were talking, and God put on our heart to give some money to this guy. God told us a certain dollar amount and we agreed. It was a going to bless and help him, we were excited to give it to him.

We said let's have him over for lunch and then we will sow the seed of money God told us to.

The Bible refers to giving money as sowing seed and it will produce a blessing and come back to you.

Luke 6:38 says *give and it will be given back to you good measure, pressed down, shaken together and running over.*

I called and asked if He could come over for lunch and told him we wanted to talk to him about something. I didn't tell him what it was about. He didn't have a clue what we were going to talk about or that we were about to bless him.

Little did we know, God had spoken to this guy's heart as well and told Him to sow a seed of money into our ministry at the same time. Neither of us knew that God had arranged this miracle to happen.

We were just doing what God told us to do and so was he. He came over for lunch and we were talking about things. Before we could tell him about the money, he asked us if he could sow a seed into our ministry.

My first thought was confusion. I was thinking, "what is happening here? We are supposed to be giving money to him!"

Before we could even sow the seed of money, we reaped money back, just like the Bible said would happen in the end times.

It would be easy to say all you guys did is exchange money, but that's not what happened at all. A lot of people don't see what God is doing because they don't understand how faith and obedience work in the kingdom of God.

God spoke to both our hearts at the same time, but neither of us knew about the other one being told to step out in faith. They were also different amounts of money.

Immediately, God spoke to my heart and reminded

me of the verse in Amos 9:13.

He showed me we just experienced a miracle; I was so excited. I read it to my wife and the single guy, and we all were amazed, WOW GOD!

It was just like the title of the story says, sowing and reaping time together.

WE ARE BLESSED TO BE A BLESSING

DOUG

In this story, I will share how God has Blessed my wife and I to be a blessing.

God wants all His children to be Blessed, to prosper, to have abundant life.

John 10:10 says Jesus came that we may receive abundant life, the devil comes to kill, steal and destroy.

God's heart is to help the hurting, sick, poor, and wounded people in the world. He wants to restore, repair, and make new.

He wants to allow us to be a part of what He is doing in the world, to be an answer to somebody's prayer. God uses people, places and things to answer your prayers!

God put on Janet's and my heart to sponsor children in Africa. About 20 years ago, we started sending monthly support to a child through Compassion International.

Our monthly support would pay for his housing, food, clothing and an opportunity to go to school. Plus, we sent him money for his birthday and Christmas.

We sponsored one child for several years, then a second child for several more years. We were sponsoring two children, and it was a joy knowing we were making a difference in someone's life.

One day God spoke to my heart and said, one day you will be supporting ten children. I thought, "wow! How can that ever happen?"

God is in the faith realm, meaning He calls us to trust Him at His word. Apart from faith, you can't please God. We are called to live by faith and walk by faith!

God was stretching our faith to do something way bigger than ourselves

He might as well have told us we would give 100,000 dollars. It would take total faith to believe and act on that word, but I knew some day it would happen somehow.

A couple years went by, and I never stopped thinking about what God spoke to me about 10 children. Finally, I told Janet, my wife, that now is the time we need to step out in faith. Let's take on three more kids bringing us to five per month. It was a step of faith we didn't have the money in our budget, but I believed God would provide somehow.

It was a couple months later, and my mom blessed us and my brother and two sisters with 5-thousand dollars each as a gift.

I thought WOW! I knew God would be faithful. I didn't have a clue how it was going to happen but in faith, we stepped out.

A year or so later, we stepped out more and took on another five children. A total step of faith, bringing the total to ten kids per month plus birthday gifts and Christmas gifts.

I didn't have a clue how God was going to make it happen. It was bigger than our budget by far.

Mark 9:23 says *All things are possible to Him who believes. Janet and I are believers!*

It is now November, a year after we took on the ten kids for monthly support and we are not behind on any bills! We have paid all our household budget and supported ten kids plus birthday and Christmas gifts. To be honest I don't even know how it happened.

God can make your money go farther than you can

by giving you favor. He helps us get good deals on purchases. We did work some overtime but not much. I really don't know how it worked out to be honest.

We are big time budget people. At the beginning of the year, I looked at our regular household expenses and our yearly income and we were going to be 6,500 dollars short. However, I said that God will provide somehow, and He did!

Now God has asked me, "why are you stopping at 10 kids?"

He said to keep stretching your faith and believe Him for more. WOW!

I'm not there yet, I'm still stretching my faith. I believe God will make it happen to help another five children.

If we are faithful in little things, God will make us ruler of much more. That's our God. He is AWESOME!

I said, God if you give me Holy Ghost inspired ideas on how to raise the extra money needed to support five more kids, I will do it.

He put on my heart to write a book about answered prayers my wife and I have experienced over the last 30 years of walking with Him.

We have had so many miracles and blessings and answered prayers. It's amazing to see God's faithfulness.

He also told me to make lamps from driftwood to sell. I love working with wood.

So that's why I'm writing this book and making lamps to sell. I am trusting God to help me earn money for five more kids.

I know and believe without a doubt God will help me bring it to pass. My goal is in one year to write a check for 2700 dollars to support five more kids, just like God told me to!

NOW WHAT

JANET

We all have those now what moments in life. What should I do? Where should I go? This door closed, what door will open?

My next story is about the NOW WHAT.

I had just finished and graduated from Caris Bible College. I was so excited that my dream of going to Bible College was now done. I was so excited and had many dreams of the possibilities to come.

I joined up with a ministry in town. It was a shelter for the homeless and it had a women's and men's program to help them recover from substance abuse. So many hurting and lost souls looking for a place to be and a new beginning. I know this all too well having come from a family where alcohol abuse was present. I also had been affected by its horrible effects on a family. I had experienced several types of abuse in my life and was once lost and hurting myself. I also had ten years of experience in the social work field. Through my journey of healing, I felt I would be a great help to the women in the women's program.

It was one of the most rewarding and challenging

experiences of my career. There were days of listening and encouraging, working with women who manipulate and learning how to help them change that behavior, setbacks and growth for all the women. I saw God work in the lives of the women who truly reached out to Him. I laughed and cried with them all. I loved them all so very deeply and wanted them all to succeed in life. I wanted them to grow and become free from the bondage they were in. I wanted them to experience all the LORD had for them, just as I had all those years ago. I wanted them to be free from the lies the enemy put in their head. They were all beautiful and have so much to offer and receive. I knew God sent them there to heal and become whole.

I was at the shelter for about 18 months pouring the message of hope, grace, and the truth of Jesus's love for them into their lives. Eventually I had the realization that my time there was coming to an end. It was so very difficult to leave for I truly loved each and every one of them. I so hoped they know that and keep that with them always.

On the day I put my 2 weeks' notice in, I struggled, but I had known it was time. I gave my notice. At the end of the day as I was driving home, I questioned God. It is ok to ask Him questions.

I said, "NOW WHAT?" I wanted to know what I was to do next, with a heavy heart. He asked me the question," What do you want to do?"

I did not hesitate, I said, "I would like to maybe work for a day center like Betty's again." I know more than spoke it and my cell phone rang. I answered the call. It was Betty, I thought this is so odd!!! She asked me what I was doing these days. I told her I just quit my job. She told me she needed to have surgery, and could I run the day center while she was recovering. I did just that. I still to this day work at the day center with Betty.

I know not all answers come that quick but this one did. God wants to give you the desires of your heart and I wanted to go back to the day center. God also knew Betty needed help. The timing was perfect, God's timing is always perfect.

CLOSE CALLS TO DEATH

DOUG

God's word tells us many things and one of those things is that God is our protector.

I will share about a couple of times God spared my life, although He has protected me many, many times!

These two stories have to do about a season of my life when I worked at a cement company as a driver of the cement trucks.

First off, I want to set the stage with truth to clear up some misunderstanding about God.

God is not the one causing the accidents in life. We all have the gift of free will and are capable of making choices, both good and bad.

Accidents happen in life. We live in a sinful, fallen world and things don't always go the right way.

Our choices and other people's choices affect each other.

God didn't create us to be robots. He gives us the ability to choose good or evil!

The good news is that God will be with us in life and He's always there to help us if we let Him.

We choose to believe His word or not. His word says that He is our protector and I believe Him! I could have died many times in life, but God has saved me.

The first story is about a large piece of cement falling on my head which could have easily killed me.

As a driver of cement trucks, one of our duties is to climb inside the truck's cement drum and chisel off the cement that's built up on the sides of the drum, which is a very dangerous job.

The cement can build up to a foot thick all around the inside of the drum and, as you probably know, cement is very heavy.

One time, I was in the drum chiseling it clean and sometimes large pieces can break off and fall wherever they want while you're right next to them. They can fall on you, so you have to choose wisely where you stand, hoping you're off to the side enough to not get hit.

I was chiseling for about a half hour, making progress. I stopped for a minute to rest and let the air clear a little, so I stepped back about a foot to rest. Then, a large piece of cement broke off and hit me on the top of my head!

It could have broken my neck and paralyzed me or worse: It could have killed me, as this piece of cement weighed several pounds.

By God's grace, I was standing just right where it glanced to the side. I went to the hospital and got stitched up, x-rayed, and eventually recovered.

The doctors said, "You're lucky to be alive, it easily could have killed you."

I say luck was not a part of this at all, for God caused me to stand back just far enough to be spared! Praise God for He is good all the time!

The second story is about an accident I had while driving the cement truck.

I was delivering a full truck load of cement. This time, it was a very heavy load.

As a driver, I knew that you have to be careful not to make any fast, sharp turns when hauling the cement because the load is very top heavy, and the truck can rollover easily.

I had to drive for about a half hour to get to the job. This early morning delivery was out in the country.

As a Christian, I talk with God throughout my day

often and pray about different things.

I was about five minutes away from arriving to my destination and I was praying, talking to God, thanking Him for all the times He has helped me in life, thanking Him for protecting me in life.

I didn't have a clue I would be needing His miraculous, life-saving power in just a couple minutes.

The road had a 90 degree turn in it and I made it around the corner, but it was an old narrow road with no shoulder at all. The front tire caught on the edge of the road and was trying to force the truck to the ditch.

I knew I couldn't react fast with the very top-heavy load, so I kept trying to get the tire back on the road but wasn't able to.

The truck started to sink more into the dirt and finally rolled completely upside down, crushing the cab where I was.

It was nothing short of a miracle that I wasn't killed in the accident, as I was hanging upside down in the truck, seat belt on.

The truck was still running so I reached up and shut it off. One of the first thoughts I thought was, "Wow

I'm still alive!" Then I thought, "I have to get out fast in case the truck catches fire." I realized the cab of the truck was crushed, so I couldn't get out either door. One side of the windshield was completely crushed, so my one and only spot I could crawl out of was to kick out the other side of the windshield.

By the Grace of God, I walked away from the accident with only minor bruises. I went to the hospital and was released with a sore neck that eventually was back to normal. I also had a small scrape on my head where I hit the roof.

The ironic part of the story is that I shared with the Highway Patrol Officer that I am a Christian and I had just prayed a couple minutes before the accident happened. I said, "I was thanking God for all the times He helped me in life and saved me, protecting me from danger."

He said, "This is a good day!"

I said, "It is? I just totaled the truck, I just about got killed and I'm probably going to get fired."

He said, "It is a good day because I don't have to put you in a body bag."

God totally answered my prayer for protection, and the Highway Patrol Officer agreed.

God doesn't always stop every accident from happening, but that doesn't mean He isn't helping us! I know He spared my life once again.

As a Christian, life isn't about luck, chance or coincidence. It's about God doing life with us and helping us amid all the dangers in life.

GOD PROVIDES FREE SAWZALL

DOUG

This story is unique. God answered a prayer that really wasn't even prayed. I will explain what I mean.

You see, God knows everything we will ever do, say, or need. He knows our whole life before we were even created in our mother's womb.

Psalm 139, I encourage you to read it. You will be amazed.

In another part of the Bible, Matthew 6, *It says your Heavenly Father knows what you need before you ask, yet other verses say it is God's pleasure to give us good gifts.*

I wanted to support more kids in Africa. At the time, my wife and I were helping to support ten kids. One day, God challenged me and spoke to my heart and said, "why not believe me for more kids, another five kids."

Wow God, you are always stretching our faith to do more than is possible in the natural, but after all, God is a supernatural God!

I told God, "I would if He would give me Holy Spirit creative ideas to earn extra money."

God took me up on the commitment. He told me to write a book about all the answered prayers He has given my wife and me.

He also knew I liked to build things with wood, so He inspired me to build lamps and other things out of driftwood to sell.

I need $2700 to pay for another five kids. I said, "God, I will write the check as soon as I get the money saved."

God is so good. We went to Duluth and gathered some driftwood for the projects. A good friend of mine was helping me get some wood.

While we were gathering wood, I mentioned to my friend Rolland that God has allowed me to purchase some power tools lately so I could build the projects. I told Rolland, "someday I need to buy a sawzall but at the time I don't have the extra money."

In all honesty, I didn't even realize I shared that with Him. I certainly wasn't asking Him for one. It was just part of my conversation at the time.

Later that night, my wife and I were spending the night at Rolland and Linda's. We were getting ready for bed and we were talking, I mentioned to Jan, my wife, I said, "someday I need to purchase a sawzall tool to cut up the driftwood but we don't have the money for it right now." Then I said out loud, "God will provide, I know He will!"

It wasn't a prayer that I even asked for, it was a declaration of the faithfulness of God. I knew He knew my need and I believed He would provide.

The next morning at breakfast Rolland said that he has a Milwaukee sawzall that he was going to give to me, WOW GOD!

You see, God provided for me before I even asked in prayer.

That's the kind of God we serve and Love, He is our Heavenly Father who gives good gifts to His children.

THE DOUBLE WAMMY AND THE BLESSING THAT FOLLOWS

JANET

One thing I can say of the LORD, is He has always been there for me. The year 2021 was a year of great trial for our nation and the world with the hit of Covid 19. I am sure we have all felt its grip of fear, sickness, and loss. I want to share my journey throughout the Pandemic.

I worked on the Covid unit at the St. Cloud Hospital also known as Medical Unit One. We had so many changes in how we cared for patients. So many unknowns, so much fear in both patients and staff. We as healthcare workers came together and fought the battle with the patients and their families. So many lives were affected by the virus. So many patients lived, and some were unfortunately lost. They will always be remembered by their loved ones and those of us who cared for them. I could continue to share all that I felt, seen and experience on the Covid unit. At this time, I want to share my personal journey.

I will start with July of 2021; I was hurt at work lifting a patient. I suffered whiplash and a concussion. I don't know if you have ever had a concussion, but when you have a concussion, your thinking and whole perception is off. I ended up in the house, sitting on my couch most of the summer. I had headaches, strange vision, I could not handle car rides, not able to read words on pages or watch tv. These things made my head hurt worse and I would get sick to my stomach. I was very depressed, confused and scared. I walked to my therapy appointments, which were a mile from my home. The funny thing was, I felt stuck in a twilight zone and did not know how bad I was. When things calmed down, my doctor was going to release me back to work for half days. I was excited.

To celebrate my being able to return to work, Doug and I drove up to Duluth for a day. We stopped at my favorite ice cream place. We were not even there ten minutes when their commercial umbrella came unattached and hit me in the head. I could not believe it. I talked with a manager to let them know I was already suffering from a concussion form work. He gave me their insurance information and told me to call them.

I went to sit by the lake on the boardwalk and

the vision in my right eye was suddenly gone. I felt confused and dazed. As time went on, I felt a severe depression come on, all in an hour. I did not understand what was wrong with me.

Needless to say, I was now suffering from a second concussion on top of the first one. I was off work for two more weeks before I could start back to half days again. I was now working with workman's compensation and the insurance for the ice cream shop. I was confused, depressed and scared again. My vison was still messed up. I heard stories of how hard it is to work with two insurance companies at the same time.

I will say, both the women I worked with - one from work comp and the other from the ice cream shop insurance - were very helpful and supportive. The compensation woman was so supportive and encouraging. I felt so blessed to have her in my life. She encouraged me and knew what to say to calm my fears. Well, now I am back to working half days, feeling grateful. I was working back on the Covid unit again.

While working my half days, my daughter, husband, and I came down with Covid. Anna got sick first. She was down and out for about a week before she started to feel better. Then Doug got sick. Being that I worked on the Covid Unit, I knew what to watch for and how to treat the symptoms at home. This was so helpful, but then I came down with Covid myself. I was sick but was not aware of how I was feeling. My focus was on Doug, because he kept getting sicker. He stopped eating and drinking. He suffered from high temperatures, coughing, and severe headaches. These were not the symptoms Anna and I had. These were the symptoms of the people who ended up in the hospital. I bought a pulse oximeter to monitor his oxygen. He was hitting below 90 into the mid 80's. I had to take him to the hospital. This was very hard for me. I could not go into the hospital with him. I had Covid and had to quarantine. I just dropped him off at the emergency entrance and waited for him to call. He was admitted to The Covid Unit. I had to trust him into God's hands and the hands of my coworkers.

Doug was on Medical Unit 1 for about four days. I was getting reports from the nurses, and I knew what the numbers meant. He was on 15 liters of O2 and could not maintain 90 percent or better. He was transferred over to Medical Progressive to receive heated high flow. I know he was getting worse, and I couldn't be there for him.

I knew when he went into the hospital it would be

a journey that may not end well. I also knew the power of prayer and that God is on our side. I know several prayer warriors and I called them all when Doug was admitted. I started a group text with them and kept them informed what was happening and what to pray for. I, for the most part, had a peace and a strength that remained with me the whole time. A strength that only God could give me.

Doug was on Medical Progressive for about three or four days. What a rollercoaster ride it was. He was so very scared. I kept watching his O2 numbers. I had a good friend who worked with me on Med 1. Her name is Terri. She became my rock along with the prayer team. She would check in with me to pray and remind me God has this. On the day before I was off quarantine, I told Doug I will be there first thing in the morning. He said he couldn't wait. I was worried about him, mostly about his thoughts and his words. He could not be calmed down. I knew he was getting worse then, and if he didn't turn around soon, he would have to go on the ventilator. At about five in the morning, I got the call. He is not improving. He is really struggling. He must go on the ventilator. WOW! What do I say? I agreed and he was on the ventilator within half an hour or less. I can't explain it but a peace came over me. I laid down and slept peacefully. I know he was resting now, and God has this.

I want to fill in some of the behind the scene things. I was sick with Covid myself. I was not sleeping well and was in continuous prayer. Each morning, starting when Doug was hospitalized, I was woken up by God at three in the morning. I was praying until peace would come. Some of the prayer team reported that they too were woken up at that time to pray as well. Terri reported being woken up in the middle of the night on several occasions to pray. My son Jeremy John and my daughter Anna were there for me. Jeremy John and my sister Joyce would visit each day. I would sit on my swing in the backyard, and they would sit six feet away on a chair. We would talk or pray. They would bring me food. They were so supportive, and I appreciate what all three of them did for me. Each night before I went to bed, Terri would call me and encourage me. I was able to rest after her call.

The morning Doug was placed on the ventilator, I went to see him. There was an amazing peace in his room. I had not seen him since I dropped him off at the emergency room door. I was told he would be on the ventilator for about three weeks. He was laying prone, on his stomach. This is to help his lungs. I stroked his hair and told him how I loved him so much. I then laid hands on him and prayed. I would read him scriptures and even sing to him. I was only allowed to stay for an hour, per hospital rules. The nurses let me stay longer some days.

Now let's talk turn around miracles. Remember, I have worked with Covid, so I know what the machine readings mean. I walked into the room on about day four or so on the ventilator. Doug was running a low-grade temp. He had not been running a temp for some time. I asked the nurse what the temp is from. He told me that he has another infection going on. He had another type of pneumonia on top of recovering from Covid. He told me that Doug will get worse before he gets better, if he gets better at all. I walked out of that room and said, "THAT IS NOT THE REPORT OF MY GOD. Doug shall live and not die and declare the goodness of the LORD in the land of the living." I also declared (Psalms 118:17), *"When the enemy comes in like a flood, the LORD raises a wall of standard against him. (Isaiah 59:19)* That wall of standard is raised. The enemy cannot take out my husband". That night at three, God woke me up as usual. This time I felt led to sing praises to God. I made up my own words and sang for several hours. It was so beautiful, so peaceful. I almost felt like the angels of God were singing with me. I believe they were. The next day when I went to see Doug, the nurse said, "He had a pretty good night." This was the first time someone said this. The other days, I was told he is the same. He did not even have the antibiotics yet. Wow God! Then a few days later, when I came to see him, he was laying on his back. That is huge!

My days I worked at the hospital, I would go see him on my break and then spend an hour or so after my shift with him. I would have the support of Terri when I grew worried or concerned. She would say things like, "God's got this! You know lots of people live and come off the ventilators. It will be okay. He will be okay." I had the continued support of Jeremy John, Anna, and Joyce. I also had the amazing prayer and worship time with my Heavenly Father each night.

The day before he came off the ventilator, they started to bring him into awareness. In other words, they wanted to wean him off. There was a wonderful respiratory tech working with him and explained the weaning process and how he was doing. I had seen her in his room for three days in a row. We watched him continue to improve. We rejoiced as he was being weaned, maintaining, and continuing to improve. She said, "Doug is my feel-good guy. When I turn down the levels on the respiratory machine, he maintains!" Watching him continuing to get better the way he did gave her hope. God is good.

On the tenth day, I went to see Doug. He was semi-alert. He could tell I was there. He could even talk a little. They told me he most likely would come off the ventilator sometime that day. I was so excited. I ask what the next step was. I was told he would be on heated high flow and go back to MPCU. Then when he improves, he will go to a regular medical unit and eventually to rehab. Praise God! I went back an hour later to check on Doug. He was sitting in a chair, talking, and on three liters of regular O2. THAT WAS HUGE. By that afternoon, he was moved to a regular bed on a medical unit, not MPCU. WOW GOD WOW!! He was on the medical unit for two and a half days and then moved to rehab. We were told he would be in rehab for two to three weeks. He was out of rehab in four days. To recap, he was on a ventilator in ICU, got off the ventilator and was home in about a week. WOW GOD!!! His total stay in the hospital was one month.

It was a journey when he came home, too. He continued to make huge improvements. I received texts from him several times a day, telling me what improvements he had. It was days of awe-struck changes in his abilities. At about two months out of the hospital, he was able to return to work. When he first went back to work, he was on a part time basis, but then eventually returned to full time work.

God helped me in every area I needed. He provided me with support from Joyce, Jeremy John, Anna, Terri and other wonderful people that came along side us and helped. Jeremy John and Anna helped with winterizing our house. God even provided the moneys needed for our monthly needs, our boat repair, and hospital debt. Doug was off work, and I was only working part time because of work comp. God worked through our friends and family. I will be forever grateful to them all. I know God will bless them all for coming along side of us and helping us through this trial.

The story continues. For several months, Doug and I continue in our individual healing. I was going to the doctor, physical therapy, and chiropractor for my concussions and whiplash. I was doing my daily exercises both for neck and my right eye. Doug continued getting stronger and healing as well. In March of 2022, I was released from my work comp case. No more PT, chiropractor, or doctor visits. I was also released form have any more eye doctor visits. This was such a release and blessing.

There was still a blessing to come that Doug and I could not have foreseen. I had to let the insurance company know I was done so we could settle the bills from the claim in Duluth. We went over what was still outstanding from that claim. That would amount to two weeks lost wages, three eye doctor appointments, one doctor visit and a chiropractor visit. Then the insurance woman totaled all of this up and said to me, "What would you like for pain and suffering?" I thought little about pain and suffering, because the past months have been a blur of emotions and survival. I told her I would be happy if she just covered the lost wages and other outstanding bills. She told me legally they must give me something for pain and suffering. I told her that whatever she feels is fair is okay with me. I had no idea what was fair or reasonable. She gave me a number that made my jaw drop. I asked if she was serious. She was. She sent me a check that wiped out all our debt except what remains on our house. Doug and I were so shocked we could not believe it. In the course of nine months, God blessed us by paying off all of his medical debt, all personal debt, continuing to heal us, and continuing to give us all the love and support we needed from our amazing friends and family. God was and is so there for us. I am so very grateful! So very grateful! I am still in awe of what God has done.

WHO DO YOU SAY I AM?

JANET

WHO DO YOU SAY I AM?   I SAY YOU ARE:

The great I Am.

You are the Alpha and the Omega, the beginning and the end.

You are LORD of lords, King of kings, the author and the finisher of my faith. You are the one true God who goes before me, beside me, behind me and in me.

You are my savior.

You are all powerful and all knowing.

You are the one who leads me and directs my path.

You are the redeemer of my soul. You are the one my soul longs for and loves. You are the lover of my soul.

You created me in your image for your great pleasure, I bring you great pleasure. Even when I fail, I bring you pleasure. My failure does not bring you pleasure but aside from my failures, I bring you pleasure.

You are the one I have right standing with. I have favor with you because I belong to you!

You hear me and are with me wherever I go and you hold me close to your heart.

You are love. You are kind. You are all knowing.

You are my very present help in times of trouble.

You are my trusted friend who is there for me, always. You are there even if I am not faithful, you remain faithful.

You are peace, joy and hope all in one.

You are my protector, provider, redeemer, comforter, hope, joy, you are the one I love with all that I am and will be. You mold and shape me with loving care. You help me to love others the way you love me, with an all-encompassing love. You teach me to hope when there seems to be no hope. As long as we are and you are, there is always the hope we have in you.

You are Father God, Holy Spirit and Jesus the Son. You are all so very much more then I can think, you are the Great I Am!

I AM

JANET

Each year at my church, the pastors go away on a retreat to hear form God. They listen for what the word for them that year will be. When they come back, some of them share their word and what it means to them. They share how it applies to the coming year and they spend the year with their focus on their word. For example, one received the word patience, another flexible and another move. Then the pastor asked us to be still and just listen and see if we got a word from God for the year. I heard a still small voice say, "I AM"! At the same time, I heard "I AM" a much deeper meaning of "I AM" resonated inside of me. It was a knowing that God is bigger and greater than anything, anyone or any situation that happens in this world or universe.

This year after Doug and I went through Covid, my two concussions and my working on the Covid unit, when I heard "I AM," a peace came over me. I had a deeper understanding of God and His unfailing love. God is always there, whether I am aware of it or not, He is there. Just as He is there with you right now in this moment in time, waiting and listening any time you want to talk. He is bigger than our pain, circumstances, anger, feeling of being lost, hopelessness or any other feeling we may have. He is the one who led me and continues to lead me through the hard times here on this earth. He was there when my mom died. He was there in all my broken relationships. He was there in my surgeries. He was there when I was afraid, lonely, lost, broken, hopeless, and in despair. He was there to help me move beyond all my hardships. He was there to work through what I need to do to live a happier, healthy life. He was there in all my life celebrations. He will continue to be there in the future. HE IS THE GREAT I AM! I have no doubt about it.

The Bible talks about Moses leading the Israelites out of Egypt. The Israelites were a people full of fear, pain, loss and hopelessness. They were in bondage to slavery. Moses was told to bring them out of Egypt by God. The people wanted to know the name of Moses's God. Moses went to God and said who do I say you are. God replied, "I AM that I AM." Here are a people in bondage for 400 years, and a man named Moses shows up and tells them he is taking them out of slavery. I know you are afraid. God will help us. This God is "I AM." He is! He led Moses to lead the people out of bondage the same way He led me out of the bondages of my life into wholeness.

I understood in church that day, when I heard the word for me is I AM. He is indeed I AM.

I encourage you to think about this. What does that mean to you? Each person has their own thoughts and experiences and beliefs as to who God is. Some of my beliefs before my life changing experience with Him were not true. I thought he was punishing me when bad things happened to me. I believed I could never be good enough. I was afraid of God and thought all the bad things that happen in this world were His fault. I thought He was just waiting for me to mess up so He could cause pain in my life. Yet I wanted to reach out to Him and I did. Even though I had these beliefs, I would talk to Him and beg Him to help when I needed help. I did not know it, but He was there helping the whole time.

When I came to a point in my life, I looked at where I came from, and the mistakes I made on my own free will, I realized others had free will as well, and their free will cause some of my pain. I also cause others pain due to my own free will. God was not to blame; He did not make others or myself do those things. We made the choice.

All those years ago, I admitted to God I made a mess of my life by my own choosing. I chose to take some wrong roads, and got hurt, by some of my choices. I chose to have relationships with people that may not have been a good choice for me. They may have been okay people, but when I was with them, I did not make good choices. I also made some poor choices as to where I would spend my time. I was a hurting young lady and I looked to fill a void in my life that only God could fill. I was wanting to fit in to be happy. I was lost and hurting, causing my own pain and sometimes I caused pain to others. I talked to God about it. I really opened up to God, even with my misunderstanding of who He is. That moment is when I asked Him to come into my life and I have never stopped following Him. I had found my place. I fit in with God. He forgave me and loved me for who I am. Through the years, I have discovered that God is merciful, kind, loving, gentle, patient, always there and so much more. He truly is the great I AM!

So back to the question I asked earlier, what does God as "I AM" mean to you? Do you want to know Him as the lover of your soul, Heavenly Father, present help in trouble, or a friend you can always rely on?

You can do like I did and come to a point in your life where you want to change your life, be healed and set free from the past, no matter how that may have looked. Do you want to be free from all the lies and come to an understanding that there is a person and a place you will always be loved and accepted and fit in? It all starts with realizing you need His help. I asked Him to lead my life. I asked Him to come into my heart, and to reveal to me who He truly is, and He showed up.

Jesus, I know I have made a mess of my life and I have blamed you for so many things. I am sorry. I need you to come into my life and rescue me and help me. I want to love you and live for you and with you. Jesus be Lord over my life show me who you are, and I will follow you the rest of my life. I want to be yours.

I said a prayer like this 37 years ago, and my life was changed forever. All THE PRAISE BE TO GOD. This is when my story changed, and my life truly began. I noticed His handprint on my life. I see Him working in my life and I am so very glad He is here for me and with me always.